The subject of the second co [...] hardly think about because we [...] [...] right now. This book could well prove to be a wake-up call for many sleepy, skeptical, and silent Christians who have little or no expectancy or understanding about the Bible's insistence that Jesus is coming soon to consummate His mission to save this world and re-create a new heaven and a new earth. I really think that RT's treatment of Jesus's parable of the ten virgins sounds like a trumpet blast to sleepy believers and could open their eyes to their responsibilities to alert and fire up their souls with an irresistible call to become all God wants us to be and do at this junction of history before it is too late. I think that it is high time that we all heard Christ's voice again, issuing a piercing alarm that can awaken us who are eager to follow Jesus so that we all recover the fact that the best is yet to come! I pray that this book will do just that.

—REV. GREG HASLAM
MINISTER, WESTMINSTER CHAPEL, LONDON

R. T. Kendall's book is totally informative about the end times. I believe his teaching of Isaac and Ishmael is absolutely right on. Certainly there is an outpouring promised that we have not seen as yet. I like the way he has us to stand in faith and not give up. I like his persistent faith pursing and knowing that what God says He does, regardless of our own timing. I've always enjoyed his books; in fact, he is my favorite contemporary author. I highly recommend this book to put on your must-read list.

—DR. MARILYN HICKEY
PRESIDENT, MARILYN HICKEY MINISTRIES

R. T. Kendall rightly calls us to hope and work for the day when the Word and Spirit will come together—and what a revival that will be!

—DR. CRAIG KEENER
PROFESSOR, NEW TESTAMENT HISTORY
ASBURY THEOLOGICAL SEMINARY

RT in his unique and brilliant way helps us anticipate and prepare for the church's greatest days on earth by urging us to be a people of the Word and the Spirit! You'll be stirred to a renewed hope and expectancy, and a greater pursuit to know God and to walk in His ways. This is RT at his best! A must-read for everyone!

—Rev. Grant Brewster
Pastor, Island Church
Bainbridge Island, Washington

A year before this book went to publication, I heard Dr. Kendall preach on the subject "The Midnight Cry," from the account of the ten virgins, Matthew 25:1–13, and I listened spellbound. I was aware I was hearing the finest exposition of this scripture that I had ever heard—and I am now eighty-five years old. Later, reading his book, I happily discovered that same holy excellence awaiting me on the printed page.

—Charles Carrin
Charles Carrin Ministries

Many of us are expecting a great move of the Holy Spirit before the second coming. RT's latest book gives great encouragement that this is coming soon. His treatment of the parable of the ten virgins provides tremendous encouragement and insight as well as a very timely warning to Christians lest they be among the foolish virgins and are shut out of this great move of God. RT is one of the clearest voices today as he clearly articulates what the Holy Spirit is saying to the church, supported by a lifetime of sound theological study and excellent Bible teaching. His ministry is a rare gift to the body of Christ. This book gives us an urgent call to "get oil" by interacting with Jesus as our glorious and beautiful Bridegroom King and to not be content to live like the foolish virgins who neglect the remarkable privilege of engaging with Him.

—Mike Bickle
International House of Prayer

This timely message of *Prepare Your Heart for the Midnight Cry* to urgently awaken the body of Christ deeply resonates within my spirit. The author's proven wisdom and stature not only makes it all the more weighty and worthy of careful attention, but it also challenges all of us who believe to fully respond to the Lord. This is an "urgent read."

—David Demian
Director, Watchman for the Nations

Thank you, RT, for restoring confidence in what is often regarded as fading doctrine. In *Prepare Your Heart for the Midnight Cry* you have restored biblical hope. You have successfully reverenced our past views without reversing our future joys. Most of all, you have refocused our souls upon the return of Christ. Come quickly, Lord Jesus!

—STEPHEN CHITTY
PASTOR, CHRISTIAN LIFE CHURCH
COLUMBIA, SOUTH CAROLINA

R. T. Kendall's latest book is both a prophetic warning and much-needed encouragement, not only to those who call themselves Charismatic or Pentecostal but also to all believers everywhere who yearn to worship God in spirit and in truth. Western Christianity, in all its forms, has struggled for centuries with the person and the work of the Holy Spirit. The contemporary work to recover a theology as well as an experienced reality of the Holy Spirit is a welcomed change to this long season due to neglect. Nonetheless, spiritual life is meant to flow within God-given banks, requiring believers to neither forsake truth in their thirst for the Spirit nor forsake the Spirit in their zeal to defend the truth. May this book become a bridge that unites them and, as it does, the often warring communities, two important spiritual components who propagate one of them against the other.

—DAN SCOTT
SENIOR MINISTER, CHRIST CHURCH
NASHVILLE, TENNESSEE

This is a daring book! In typical Kendall style, RT walks in "where angels fear to tread."

This book is a stirring book. If the reader has settled into a comfortable eschatology with most things about the future assumed, it will prove bothersome. You are apt to disagree with some of it, agree with much of, and be puzzled with the rest of it.

This book is a biblical book. I have not, in my memory, seen a book more frequently referring to the Scriptures. This is because RT is a "Word" man. He believes the Bible to be the Holy Spirit's premium product and our unerring guide. He has been a Word man from the get-go, but one day long ago he became a Word-Spirit man, and the rest is history.

Finally this book is a necessary book. Don't allow an early disagreement to rob you of the whole message of this splendid book. Hold all conclusions until you have read through to the last page.

—JACK TAYLOR
PRESIDENT, DIMENSIONS MINISTRIES
MELBOURNE, FLORIDA

In this book, *Prepare Your Heart for the Midnight Cry*, R. T. Kendall urges the faithful believers to live in the light of the imminence of Christ's return. This type of expectant living does not cause us to put on white robes and head for the mountains. Indeed, the opposite is true as Jesus said we are to "occupy till He comes." This book will sober you up if you are tempted to go into a spiritual coma.

—MICHAEL YOUSSEF, PhD
AUTHOR, *END TIMES AND THE SECRET OF THE MAHDI*

I have great respect and appreciation for my dear friend R. T. Kendall. I've known him for many years now. I am so happy to recommend his amazing book *Prepare Your Heart for the Midnight Cry*. Without question you will be called to ponder and explore new vistas concerning the end-time plans of Father God.

RT does a masterful job of unfolding the parable of the ten virgins; it is extremely exciting and insightful. Much is discovered by his keen revelations of how Christ our Lord used earthly stories to display heavenly truths. You will be greatly blessed by this book. You will discover that "the best is yet to come!"

—BOBBY CONNER
EAGLES VIEW MINISTRIES
www.bobbyconner.org

RT's latest book, *Prepare Your Heart for the Midnight Cry*, invites the church, which was born to blossom and bless, to not settle for a former glory but to wake up from her slumber and ooze the life-giving nectar of the kingdom. This book is a rally cry: with refreshing honesty, thoroughly biblical content, and compellingly articulateness RT invites us to take heed and hold of the greatest need of the church today. This book not only declares RT's stellar commitment to sound doctrine and his openness to the Spirit, but it also demonstrates his deep integrity and a man whose heart is to see the God of the Bible made famous. A poignant and much-needed prophetic voice for this generation and the generations to come.

—Rob Wall
Curate, Holy Trinity Brompton, London

My friend R. T. Kendall is a powerful voice in this generation. He teaches with authority and clarity, and his writings never fail to inspire and inform. *Prepare Your Heart for the Midnight Cry* is no exception. RT's conviction in this book that the next great move of God on earth will be far greater than anything we have seen up until now is a very compelling one.

—Matt Redman
Songwriter, United Kingdom

R. T. Kendall's *Prepare Your Heart for the Midnight Cry* is compelling, challenging, and courageous, which provokes much contemplation and confidence in Christ's return.

—Rev'd. Canon J. John
Author, Speaker, and Director,
Philo Trust

It is indeed inspiring that such a well-known and respected leader as Dr. R. T. Kendall would not only write about the soon return of King Jesus but also clearly teach that the mightiest move of the Holy Spirit ever is imminent and pending. Read this book, and buy oil!

—John Arnott
Catch The Fire, Toronto

R. T. Kendall predicts a soon-coming worldwide revival, and I am sure he is right. The Midnight Cry will enliven our hopes and prayers. We are to expect the discipling of all nations (not "a few in all nations"!), and RT's vision for the future is surely what is predicted in the optimistic passages of Scripture (Isaiah 2; Micah 5; Psalm 72; Romans 11;

Ephesians 4:13–16; maybe Hebrews 3:9 and Revelation 20—and RT would add the parable of the ten virgins!). With the current moving around of vast populations among the nations, it certainly looks as if the day is drawing near—but we are warned about some suffering along the way! Certainly *Prepare Your Heart for the Midnight Cry* enlivens our hopes and prayers.

—Dr. Michael Eaton
Nairobi, Kenya

I was present when RT first gave his talk about the Word and Spirit coming together. His new book is an elaboration of that prophetic word, which he finds in the parable of the ten virgins. It is a timely warning to the church generally to wake us up and be ready for what is coming down the road. Like all prophetic writings, this book should be read and weighed. RT writes with passion and conviction. One may not agree with all his conclusions, but one thing is outstanding: he holds together the Spirit and the Word as well as anyone I know.

—Ken Costa
Churchwarden
Holy Trinity Brompton, London

"When disaster comes to a city, has not the LORD caused it? Surely the Sovereign LORD does nothing without revealing his plan to his servants the prophets" (Amos 3:6–7, NIV). R. T. Kendall is a proven and reliable prophet for our time, deeply steeped in Bible revelation and personal communication with our God. Some may question his message (I do not) because it seems frightening—but "as in the days of Noah," the alarm was a mighty blessing to those who heeded it. And so *Prepare Your Heart for the Midnight Cry* is to us; we do well to heed and be prepared. Thank you for your faithfulness, Brother Kendall.

—Pat Boone
Actor and Author

R. T. Kendall is a man for all seasons with a varied background and international ministry among Pentecostals and Charismatics. His new book, *Prepare Your Heart for the Midnight Cry*, is a call for a new outpouring of the Holy Spirit that every Spirit-filled believer longs to see. May it be so.

—VINSON SYNAN
DEAN EMERITUS
REGENT UNIVERSITY SCHOOL OF DIVINITY

The Christian message to most of us is great but complicated. Jesus tried to explain the essence of His rabbinic message by telling stories in true rabbinic fashion; one such story is that of the ten virgins. It is a story of the grace of God that I have never truly understood. Then RT turns up and shows truths and reality of the parable that I have never truly understood, but now they are made real. My father took me as a child regularly to see RT. As an adult I regularly took him to see the Middle East extremists that I worked with, such as Yasser Arafat. Over the years RT and I have become true friends, but I still learn from his biblical teaching and amazing and incredible insight.

Read this book, and you too will be anointed and inspired by God through His servant RT.

—THE REV'D. CANON DR. ANDREW P. B. WHITE
PRESIDENT, FOUNDATION FOR RELIEF AND
RECONCILIATION IN THE MIDDLE EAST (FRRME)

Once again Dr. Kendall has provided an extensive and well-researched piece of literature, deeply rooted in Scripture and ready to shake nations. *Prepare Your Heart for the Midnight Cry* brings explanation to the pending collision of Word and Spirit, and an expectation for something that has been separated for far too long. This book will give readers a greater level of anticipation and readiness to welcome the second coming of Christ.

—BILL WILSON
METRO WORLD CHILD

Imagine all of Christendom awakened from centuries-long sleep, and half of that number (over a billion strong) with lights burning bright, giving witness to the second coming of Jesus. *Prepare Your Heart for the Midnight Cry* enables Christianity to shed the eschatological scales from our eyes and become again the bold, expectant, hopeful light of the world. My father, the late Rev. Billy Ball, often said in his preaching, "The last thing a sleeping man wants to hear is an alarm clock!" May R. T. Kendall's articulate and inspiring work on this parable be part of that blessed sound that inaugurates the "greatest awakening" as the enemies of Christ become His footstool, culminating in the triumphant return of Jesus Christ!

—Rev. Terry Ball
Pastor, First Church of God
Monroe, Ohio

Having heard Dr. R. T. Kendall preach on the Midnight Cry, I had no doubt it would become a book. In fact, *Prepare Your Heart for the Midnight Cry* is a must-read for everyone who cries aloud maranatha (O Lord, come!), sobs quietly for the Lord's return, or questions its truth.

—David D. Ireland, PhD
Senior Pastor
Author, *Raising a Child Who Prays*
www.DavidIreland.org

PREPARE YOUR HEART

FOR THE

MIDNIGHT CRY

PREPARE YOUR HEART
FOR THE
MIDNIGHT CRY

R. T. KENDALL

CHARISMA
HOUSE

PREPARE YOUR HEART FOR THE MIDNIGHT CRY by R. T. Kendall
Published by Charisma House
Charisma Media/Charisma House Book Group
600 Rinehart Road
Lake Mary, Florida 32746
www.charismahouse.com

Cover design by Vincent Pirozzi
Design Director: Justin Evans

Visit the author's website at www.rtkendallministries.com.

Library of Congress Cataloging-in-Publication Data:
Names: Kendall, R. T., 1935- author.
Title: Prepare your heart for the midnight cry / R.T. Kendall.
Description: First edition. | Lake Mary : Charisma House, 2016. | Includes
   bibliographical references and index.
Identifiers: LCCN 2016030832| ISBN 9781629986241 (trade paper : alk.
paper) |
   ISBN 9781629986258 (e-book)
Subjects: LCSH: Ten virgins (Parable) | Bible. Matthew, XXV,
1-13--Criticism,
   interpretation, etc. | End of the world--Biblical teaching. | Second
   Advent--Biblical teaching.
Classification: LCC BT378.T4 K46 2016 | DDC 243--dc23
LC record available at https://lccn.loc.gov/2016030832

17 18 19 20 21 — 9 8 7 6 5 4 3 2
Printed in the United States of America

In honor of my first mentor
The Rev. Dr. Billy T. Ball (1927–2015)

CONTENTS

FOREWORD

I FIRST MET DR. R. T. KENDALL AT A BREAKFAST MEETING twenty-five years ago. At that time he was the minister of the prestigious Westminster Chapel, situated just around the corner from Buckingham Palace, and I had recently been appointed as senior pastor of Kensington Temple, the Elim Pentecostal Church located in London's Notting Hill Gate. Our meeting had been arranged by a mutual friend, Lyndon Bowring, who sensed that there was a spiritual connection between the Evangelicalism of Westminster Chapel and the Pentecostalism of Kensington Temple.

During the breakfast RT leaned over the table and said pointedly, "Colin, you need my theology," then paused and added, "I need your anointing!" A long-standing friendship was established. From that moment we have been in constant prayer for one another, taking a keen interest in one another's ministries as well as learning from and challenging one another.

Over the years RT has helped me grow in my understanding of the Scriptures. I have also seen his openness to the Spirit. I recall his introduction to Rodney Howard-Browne, the Kansas City Prophets, and other highly controversial elements of Charismatic Christianity. In search of God's glory, RT does not want to leave any stone unturned, but he remains prepared to critique what he finds, never losing his exegetical conscience and theological awareness.

The two key elements in RT's spiritual passion are the Word and the Spirit working in tandem. This is biblical Christianity of course, and to help promote the idea, RT organized a Word and Spirit conference in Wembley in 1992. During the conference he created quite a stir when he said that the Charismatic movement was "Ishmael," not the final promise, but that "Isaac" was on the way. Most of my Charismatic and

Pentecostal friends were offended by RT's apparent identification of them with Ishmael, to their minds a symbol of fleshly religion as opposed to genuine spiritual Christianity.

However, I understood clearly what RT had in mind. He saw something greater than the twentieth-century outpourings of the Spirit that gave rise to the Pentecostal, Charismatic, and Third Wave movements. These have brought great spiritual benefit and impact to the world. They comprise the second largest identifiable Christian grouping in existence today. However, just as Ishmael was not the fulfillment of God's promise to Abraham, so RT was saying we must look beyond what we have today and expect "Isaac," a far greater move of the Holy Spirit than we have ever seen before.

The idea of the Word and the Spirit coming together in a great move of God has been around in Pentecostal circles for some time. A long-standing prophecy of Pentecostal pioneer Smith Wigglesworth has been frequently quoted: "When the Word and Spirit combine, we shall see the greatest move the church of Jesus Christ has ever seen." I am grateful to RT for helping clarify what can be safely attributed to Wigglesworth and what we can assume are later embellishments. The source for this quote is strong. George Stormont, whom I had the privilege of meeting early in my Christian experience, was close to Wigglesworth and was known to be a man of the Spirit and integrity of heart. He was among the first to make the words of this prophecy widely known. Of course, as responsible believers we do not take modern-day prophetic words as infallible. The identification of Isaac with the final move of God preparing both the church and the world for the second coming of Jesus rests on clear biblical arguments.

It would be hard to claim that what we have seen so far is the final move of God on the earth. Each successive revival in history adds to what went before and prepares for what is to come. But the last move of God will finally prepare the world for the return of Jesus Christ. It is going to happen, and if RT is right, it is going to happen soon!

Leaving precise timing aside, we know that Christ is going to manifest His presence in the church before He comes back to claim her as His bride. Romans chapter 11 speaks of the coming fullness of Israel and the nations, and as Andrew Murray makes clear, this indicates a mass turning of Jew and Gentile to Christ before the return of Christ. Either these events will unfold rapidly as RT suspects, or they will play out gradually and continually until everything is fulfilled. I tend to agree with RT. The age will climax in a series of critical, even cataclysmic events. The Midnight Cry is the key experience that sets the others in motion.

The linking of this Midnight Cry in Matthew 25 with the end-time revival was new to me. I had never identified the wedding banquet mentioned in this parable of Jesus with the final move of God on the earth. I had never thought to connect the waking of the wise and foolish virgins to the end-time awakening of the church and the subsequent spiritual awakening of the nations—until, that is, I noticed one day an article by RT posted on his blog. He outlined the basic idea of the Midnight Cry. I was excited to read what he had to say. Here was a man, a prominent Evangelical open to the Spirit, giving shape to an important idea that I have long pondered and preached on many times. RT elaborated his exposition in a series of gripping sermons he preached at Kensington Temple in the first half of 2014.

I believe that the way RT exegetes Matthew 25 is correct and, at the very least, provides us with an interesting scriptural analogy building on what we know from other passages. The parable of the wise and foolish virgins presents some unique insights into the time immediately preceding the return of Christ. By and large the contemporary church is asleep, but we know from Revelation 22:17 that this will not always be the case. The Spirit is going to awaken the bride of Christ to His imminent return. He is going to do it through the Midnight Cry.

RT's desire is that this book will itself be a mini wake-up call to the church. I certainly found it disturbing. The scary thing is that no destinies will be changed by the Midnight Cry. We will be awakened to the reality of the lives we have chosen to live, the choices we have made which will have defined our destiny. We can change this now, but we will not be able to change it then. Those who read this book and take its central message seriously may find a new spirituality rising in them.

Historically those Christians most used and owned by God have often demonstrated a keen eschatological awareness. Certainly the very early Christians lived that way.

RT hopes to evoke in his readers a renewed expectancy of the return of Christ and an eagerness to be a part of the end-time move of the Spirit. The greatest days of the church lie ahead, maybe just ahead. In any case, we must all embrace the central message of the parable of the wise and foolish virgins. We must be ready; we must be watchful. Taking these matters seriously now will mean that we will be ready then and will not miss out on the greatest move of God in the church since that described in the Acts of the Apostles. This present book is an important call to the church of today to prepare for the events that lie ahead.

—REV. COLIN DYE, SENIOR MINISTER
KENSINGTON TEMPLE, LONDON, ENGLAND

At that time the kingdom of heaven will be like ten virgins who took their lamps and went out to meet the bridegroom. Five of them were foolish and five were wise. The foolish ones took their lamps but did not take any oil with them. The wise ones, however, took oil in jars along with their lamps. The bridegroom was a long time in coming, and they all became drowsy and fell asleep.

At midnight [Gr. *mesees de nuktos*—"middle of night"] the cry rang out: "Here's the bridegroom! Come out to meet him!"

Then all virgins woke up and trimmed their lamps. The foolish ones said to the wise, "Give us some of your oil; our lamps are going out."

"No," they replied, "there may not be enough for both us and you. Instead, go to those who sell oil and buy some for yourselves."

But while they were on their way to buy the oil, the bridegroom arrived. The virgins who were ready went in with him to the wedding banquet. And the door was shut.

Later the others also came. "Lord, Lord," they said, "open the door for us!"

But he replied, "Truly I tell you, I don't know you."

Therefore keep watch, because you do not know the day or the hour.

—MATTHEW 25:1–13, NIV

PROLOGUE

A MAN GETTING READY TO JUMP OFF THE GOLDEN GATE BRIDGE in San Francisco was spotted by an Evangelical Christian. The Christian rushed to him and said, "Oh, sir, please don't jump. Don't you believe in God?"

"Yes, as a matter of fact I do believe in God," the man replied.

"Oh, good. I too believe in God. Tell me, are you a Jew or Gentile?"

"I'm a Gentile."

"I too am a Gentile. Oh, sir, please don't jump. May I ask, are you a Christian or a Muslim?"

"I'm a Christian."

"This is amazing. I too am a Christian. May I ask, are you Protestant or Catholic?"

"I'm a Protestant."

"Praise the Lord. I'm so glad to get to you in time. I'm a Protestant. Tell me, are an Evangelical or a liberal?"

"I am an Evangelical."

"Praise the Lord. Thank You, Jesus. But do tell me, might you be a Baptist or Presbyterian?"

"I'm a Baptist."

"This is most extraordinary. I too am a Baptist. I'd be interested to know—are you a Southern Baptist or an Independent Baptist?"

"I am an Independent Baptist."

"This is almost too good to be true," the Christian continued. "I am also an Independent Baptist. Do forgive me, but I must ask: are you a premillennialist, an amillennialist, or a postmillennialist?"

"I am a premillennialist."

"This is extraordinary; it is so obvious the Lord sent me here to stop you in the nick of time from taking your life. I too am solidly a premillennialist. But could I just ask one more question: are you a pre-tribulationist, midtribulationist, or posttribulationist?"

"I'm a posttribulationist."

"Jump, you heretic."

PREFACE

I HOPE THE APOCRYPHAL STORY IN MY PROLOGUE MADE YOU SMILE. If it did, you will likely know how the finer points of eschatology can sometimes make people extremely divisive and even very emotional. I have not written this book to convince you of all the details of my interpretation of the parable of the ten virgins. It has taken me more than sixty years to arrive at the position taken in this book. No two people have ever agreed on the minute details of events leading up to the second coming. I certainly do not propose to be the first to have gotten it right!

Here is what I know for sure: that we should heed Jesus's words: "Let your waist be girded *and your lights be burning*" (Luke 12:35, emphasis added). My treatment of the parable of the ten virgins is presented with the hope you will do just that, and that it will bring you to a closer walk with God. I urge you to get ready for what I believe is coming soon.

To put it another way, the purpose of this book is to warn of the coming Midnight Cry and to show how you may be sure you are *not* like the foolish virgins in the parable. Once the Midnight Cry comes, it will be too late to cross over from being a foolish virgin to a wise virgin. But it is not too late *now*.

This book is essentially my exposition and interpretation of the parable of the ten virgins in Matthew 25:1–13.

There are at least two ways of viewing most parables of Jesus. The first is simply to give one single lesson of each of them and leave it there. For example, we could deal with the parable of the ten virgins in one stroke and say that it merely shows the importance of being ready for the Midnight Cry and the sad consequences of not being ready—nothing more. But I believe there is more to be said about it than that. One might explain even the parable of the sower in a sentence or two by saying it shows that not all who hear the Word of God receive it the same way; some persevere, some don't. But since Jesus explained the parable of the sower in some detail (Matt. 13:18–23)—as He did also with the parable of the weeds (Matt. 13:36–43), I conclude that He could have easily done this with other parables as well. I certainly wish He had explained the parable of the ten virgins in more detail! He didn't, so we do our best to grasp it and apply it. Because Matthew brought in this parable in the context of the very last days (Matt. 24) and the final judgment (Matt. 25:31–41), I conclude that the parable of the ten virgins is an eschatological parable. *Eschatology* simply means "doctrine of last things"; for example, the last days, signs of the times, second coming, judgment, heaven, and hell.

In my book *The Parables of Jesus* I state that one must not try to make a parable stand evenly on "all four legs." That means one must be cautious in trying to make every nuance of a parable have a special meaning. And yet it is not always easy to know which part of a parable needs to be applied in a specific way.

THE FIRST WORD AND SPIRIT CONFERENCE: OCTOBER 1992

In my closing address at our first Word and Spirit Conference at London's Wembley Conference Centre in October 1992 I gave a prophetic analogy. The talk can be found verbatim as "The Post-Charismatic Era" in a book by Paul Cain and me called *The Word and the Spirit*. To summarize: I called the Pentecostal/Charismatic movement "Ishmael" and stated that "Isaac is coming," the latter being the greatest move of the Holy Spirit since Pentecost. This book you now hold in your hands is not only an elaboration of that original talk but also an extension of the chapter called "Isaac" in my recent book called *Holy Fire*.

I had wanted to call the present book "Isaac" but decided instead to call it as you now see it, *Prepare Your Heart for the Midnight Cry*.

My talk at Wembley caused a bit of a furor. I did not anticipate this, but I should have. Although some major leaders accepted my analogy immediately, some were less than pleased. "You called us Ishmael," one good friend said curtly to me. And yet I could see why he was offended.

Some people who had given their lives and risked their reputations for being a part of the Pentecostal/Charismatic movement certainly did not feel very affirmed by my talk. This movement claims some six hundred million converts, and some would say there are many more than that.

This prophetic analogy is merely my way of explaining part of God's unveiling purpose in contemporary history. If you were offended by my Ishmael-Isaac analogy, I hope that at least one benefit of this present book will result in convincing you that it is certainly *not* a put-down of Pentecostals and Charismatics (of whom I am one) but rather a way to illustrate that *the best is yet to come*. That said, one of the leaders of the Pentecostal movement, knowing my views, wrote to me recently: "I believe we are living in the great awakening before the rapture. It is the Pentecostal/Charismatic movement." In other words, according to him, what we have at the moment is as good as it gets. And yet another well-known leader wrote to me saying, "I'm one of those Pentecostal/ Charismatics who have often said, 'If this is all there is, I'm disappointed.' Rather than being offended by the comparison to Ishmael, I'm eager for another outpouring, and being a lover of both the Word and the Spirit, nothing delights me more than a marriage of the two." I can only add that, in my opinion, if what we have at the moment is all we can ever expect, the outlook for the church is very bleak indeed. But there *is* more to come!

What you will read in this book is an unfolding of my conviction regarding the next great and—in my view—*final* move of God on the earth. It is an elaboration of the chapter called "Isaac" in my book *Holy Fire*. Once in a while a chapter needs more attention—and becomes an entire book, like the chapter "Total Forgiveness" in *God Meant It for Good*; it became my book *Total Forgiveness*. Although I have been humbly gratified by a good number of Charismatic and Pentecostal leaders endorsing *Holy Fire*, I need to say a lot more about the combination of the Word and Spirit to demonstrate that the greatest movement of the Holy Spirit since Pentecost is coming soon. I will also show in more detail in chapter 1 that as the promise to Abraham concerning Isaac's future was greater than the promise about Ishmael, so also will the next great move of the Holy Spirit be infinitely greater than the blessing that has come through the Pentecostal/Charismatic movement.

It is my view that the Word and the Spirit coming together simultaneously is an important part of the parable of the ten virgins. The Midnight Cry will come in the *middle of the night*, metaphorically speaking—when the church is in a deep sleep.

I have dedicated this book to my first mentor, the Rev. Dr. Billy T. Ball. I was privileged to speak at his funeral in December 2015. He was the first to help open the parable of the ten virgins to me. Not a little of what I say in this book comes from what he taught me.

There have been a host of friends—too many to mention—who have given me considerable input and some valuable criticisms. I have done my best to take them all on board. I thank Colin Dye, senior pastor of Kensington Temple, for writing the foreword. He was present at the first Word and Spirit Conference in 1992 and possibly the only major Charismatic leader at the time to embrace my Ishmael-Isaac analogy.

Warmest thanks to my editor Debbie Marrie for being possibly my greatest encourager in writing this book. Thank you, Debbie, for your patience in waiting for the final manuscript—due almost two years ago! Thank you too for your wisdom and guidance in editing my material. Two people who were under my ministry at Westminster Chapel have given me tremendous input. I owe a special debt of gratitude to Philip Evans. He has given very helpful suggestions concerning my book and has spent countless hours researching the origin of Smith Wigglesworth's famous alleged prophecy to which I refer in chapter 2. Secondly, one of our deacons during those years, Paul Gardiner, was present at the previously mentioned Word and Spirit Conference in 1992. He has graciously spent an amazing amount of time reading the manuscript and has offered invaluable suggestions. Finally, my deepest thanks goes to my wife, Louise—my best friend and critic—for her continuous encouragement to me in writing this book.

As for the comparison between Ishmael and Isaac, "you ain't seen nothing yet," as the saying goes. Indeed, in the words of the poet Robert Browning, I guarantee that "the best is yet to be."

INTRODUCTION

IN THE 1960s THE BEATLES FAMOUSLY BOASTED THAT THEY WERE "more popular than Jesus." And they were certainly right about that. What is more, the situation sadly is much worse today than it was then.

My ambition is to make the God of the Bible famous all over the world. When we pray the petition in the Lord's Prayer, "Hallowed be Your name," we are praying for the name of God to be hallowed, or honored, all over the world.

A day when God is famous all over the world is coming. It is an era coming soon. It is what the Old Testament prophets called the "day of the LORD" (e.g., Joel 2:31).

As John the Baptist preceded the ministry of Jesus, so will the Midnight Cry precede the second coming of Jesus. The earliest message of the New Testament was to flee from the coming wrath of God (Matt. 3:7). This shook the whole of Judaism from the Jordan River to Jerusalem. The Midnight Cry will likewise wake up the church—but all around the world. It will herald the soon coming of Jesus. The Midnight Cry will bring about a sudden and effectual awakening of the church, resulting in a restoration of the fear of God in the church and also the world. This will be the consequence of the coming of the Holy Spirit in ever-increasing power, which Jesus will orchestrate from His throne at the right hand of God. This will restore the Word and Spirit to the level it was in the earliest days of the church. This will prepare the bride of Christ for His coming.

All this will happen in a short period of time. And it is coming soon.

THE DAY OF THE LORD

Anytime you see the "Midnight Cry" or "Cry" capitalized in this book, you will know I am referring to what I believe is the next major event on God's calendar. It will initiate the era known as the Day of the Lord, which will culminate in the return of Jesus to this planet. The Midnight Cry will therefore take place *prior* to the second coming of Jesus. As God the Father alone knows the day and the hour of the second coming (Matt. 24:36), so also does He know the exact time of the Midnight Cry. This Cry will bring about an unprecedented awakening in the church and will spread quickly all over the world. Indeed, everyone in the church and everyone outside of it will eventually be affected from head to toe by the fear of the Lord. The impact and result of this Cry will be much greater and far wider than the event that took place on September 11, 2001. It will come in the middle of the night, metaphorically speaking—at which time virtually no one is expecting it, when the church is in a deep, deep sleep.

It could come any day. I think it is highly possible I will see it in my lifetime. I literally look for the beginnings of it every day.

THE STAGES OF GOD'S END-TIME EVENTS

Before I go any further, I need to explain that I believe the next two events on God's calendar will each unfold in two stages. In this book I will show that there are two phases of the Midnight Cry: (1) a wake-up call to the church followed by (2) the greatest revival since Pentecost, or "Isaac." I will also show that there are two phases of the second coming: (1) the greatest revival since Pentecost, or "Isaac," followed by (2) the final judgment.

It may help you to refer to this simple table as a reference.

The Midnight Cry	The Second Coming
Stage one: wake-up call	Stage one: great revival; "Isaac"; Jesus's spiritual coming
Stage two: great revival; "Isaac"; Jesus's spiritual coming	Stage two: final judgment; Jesus's physical coming

You will see that phase two of the Midnight Cry and phase one of the second coming are exactly the same. This is because the initial wake-up call will *lead to* the great revival that makes the bride ready. At what point the wake-up call becomes the great revival—namely, the spiritual coming of Christ—is hard to predict. John the Baptist gave the wake-up call to Israel before Jesus's ministry became center stage. John the Baptist faded away while the ministry of Jesus took over. John said that Jesus must increase while he decreases (John 3:30). In much the same way the wake-up call to the church will mature toward solid teaching—this being the ultimate fulfillment of the Word and Spirit coming together. Shortly after the wake-up call to the church, then, there will come the greatest outpouring of the Spirit in the history of the church. This revival will be orchestrated by Jesus Christ Himself at the right hand of God.

The second coming of Jesus therefore will be in two phases. Phase one: the *spiritual* coming of Jesus, namely, when Jesus remains seated at the right hand of the Father and sends the Spirit of God in great power to the church. This will result in Him making His enemies His footstool. This, as I said, is when the bride of Christ makes herself ready, as described in Revelation 19:7: "For the marriage of the Lamb has come, and His wife has made herself ready." Phase two will be the *physical* coming of Jesus, when He leaves His position at the right hand of God, *having made* His enemies His footstool, and sets up the final judgment—called the judgment seat of Christ. In other words, Jesus will not physically leave His position at the right hand of God until He makes His enemies His footstool.

This book is about the coming Day of the Lord—introduced by the Midnight Cry. Part 1 of this book (chapters 1 and 2) will be an explanation of my prophetic analogy. Part 2 (chapters 3–15) is the main part of the book; it is my exposition of the parable of the ten virgins (Matt. 25:1–13). This section pertains to the church and its readiness for the Midnight Cry. Part 3 (chapters 16–20) is an introduction to what the New Testament teaches regarding the second coming of Jesus to judge the entire world. I suspect that many Christians have not thought through for themselves what they believe about the second coming. Most probably only know what they have heard from one or two sermons—or, perhaps, from reading the novel or seeing the movie *Left Behind*. I felt my book would be incomplete without this overview of basic eschatology. The essential point is that Jesus will not leave His throne at the right hand of the Father until He makes all His enemies His footstool (Ps. 110:1; Acts 3:21).

MY VISION OF THE MIDNIGHT CRY

In 1956 I had a vision that there would be a worldwide awakening before the second coming. For some sixty years I have believed that the Midnight Cry of Matthew 25:6 indicates an awakening that *precedes* the second coming of Jesus Himself. Before then I followed the popular line that "midnight" meant twelve o'clock midnight on God's calendar—as if the end of history—when the second coming would take place. But the Greek indicates something different:

> But at midnight [Gr. *mesees de nuktos*—middle of night] there was a cry, "Look, the bridegroom is coming! Come out to meet him!"
> —MATTHEW 25:6

A number of friends have lovingly cautioned me that—so they thought—my view of Matthew 25:6 has no precedent in the history of biblical exegesis. I admit that this worried me a bit. But it turns out that these friends were wrong this time. My interpretation has several precedents. For one, the esteemed teacher Henry Alford (1810–1871) made the same point, this being the centerpiece of my book. Alford was probably the most respected exegetical Greek scholar in the nineteenth century. He was favored by Charles H. Spurgeon in his day. Said Henry Alford: "The warning cry [of Matthew 25:6] is *before* the coming"[1] (Alford's italics), this being the crucial exegetical point I have to make. I am *not* claiming Alford to have taught all I propose in this book. There are many others too who take this view. This simply demonstrates that the idea of a gap in time between the "Cry" and the coming of the Bridegroom is not new.

Some will ask: How much time is there between the Midnight Cry and the physical second coming of Jesus? I don't know. I only know that a lot can happen between these two events. God can do a lot in a very short period of time. The eventual result will be the fulfillment of ancient prophecies that the knowledge of the glory of the Lord will cover the earth as the waters cover the seas (Hab. 2:14).

People have asked me whether my position fits a particular eschatological scheme—premillennial (Jesus coming *before* the thousand-year reign described in Revelation 20:2–7—the view of many fundamentalists), postmillennial (Jesus coming *after* the thousand years—the view of many Puritans), or amillennial (that the one thousand years in Revelation 20:2–7 is not to be taken literally—the view of many Reformed Evangelicals). My answer: I don't know. I only believe that the greatest outpouring of the Holy Spirit since the Day of Pentecost is at hand. Among other things, this coming of the Spirit will result in: (1) the clearest preaching and teaching of the gospel of Jesus Christ seen since the days of the early church and (2) the gospel being accompanied by signs and wonders not seen since the days of the earliest church.

My late friend John Paul Jackson told me about a vision he had many years ago. Among other things he saw in this vision, John Paul indicated that the key to the next great move of God will be *the Book of Romans and especially Romans 4*. This means there will be a restoration of the teaching of justification by faith alone as taught by the Reformers but also a clarification of what the New Testament teaches about our inheritance. If John Paul's vision was indeed from the Spirit of God, it is thrilling that a renewed love for the Book of Romans is coming.

The time between the Midnight Cry and the second coming of the person of Jesus will be like living in the Book of Acts. But more than that, as I said above, this will be the time when the bride of Christ makes herself "ready" (Rev. 19:7). This is when our Lord Jesus Christ will have made all His enemies His "footstool" as prophesied in Psalm 110:1.

To summarize: first comes the Midnight Cry—in two phases; after that, the second coming takes place in two phases: Jesus's spiritual coming and His physical coming.

SHIFTING OF GEARS

Before writing this book, I have preached this basic message over twenty times in several places in the world. I have sought always to recognize that (1) this teaching will be new to some people, (2) I certainly do not wish to ram it down anyone's throat, and (3) I ask that they will consider prayerfully a perspective that, hopefully, will make sense to them. I realize it will mean shifting a lot of gears in many people's thinking.

But now for the bad news. I'm sorry, but this awakening will be accompanied with severe suffering, and in many places there will be unthinkable persecution. Do not forget what happened to John the Baptist (Mark 6:14–29), to Stephen (Acts 7:54–60), and to James the brother of John (Acts 12:2). Some will die as martyrs for the faith. We all have been reading about unprecedented manifestations of evil in the world. But do not think these will be limited to the Middle East. Such evil will spread to every nation in which there are Christians, including the United Kingdom, other countries in Europe, and the United States. Some will experience horrible deaths. While I was writing this book, there occurred the terrorist attacks in Paris and Brussels.

The church will also go through horrible persecution. I wish it were not so. Indeed, the examples of suffering and pain in places like Iraq and Syria will widen. The time will come that wherever a Christian may be found, there will be the perpetual threat of persecution, suffering, and untimely death.

Some will ask: Where is the rapture—when Christians are caught up to meet the Lord in the air—in this scheme? I'm afraid this is an ill-posed question. This question assumes the validity of a popular teaching about the second coming—as in the film *Left Behind*—that Christians will be "raptured" before great tribulation comes and they will be spared of terrible suffering. I cut my teeth on this perspective. I know it backward and forward. Although my change of mind did not come overnight, I gradually came to see that this teaching—particularly as outlined by the *Scofield Reference Bible*—is without a solid foundation in Holy Scripture. This is one the reasons I have written part 3 in this book. It is my view that the church will suffer horrible tribulation in some places—if not virtually everywhere. It has already begun in some parts of the globe. As I will show, the church being taken up to meet the Lord in the clouds actually takes place simultaneously with the physical coming of Jesus to be the Supreme Judge. The notion that Christians will be raptured out of great suffering is, I fear, one more ingredient that will keep Christians in a deep sleep. The next thing on God's calendar, then, is not the rapture but the Midnight Cry preceding the second coming of Christ.

The awakening of the church as a result of the Midnight Cry will result in millions of conversions and many undoubted signs and wonders. Hundreds of thousands of people in America and Britain, for example, who never went to church will be saved. Millions of Muslims will be converted virtually overnight. The blindness on Israel will be lifted, and millions of Jews and Israelis will acknowledge that Jesus of Nazareth is their true Messiah. It will be the greatest wedding banquet ever, namely being right in the middle of that greatest move of the Spirit since Pentecost. But not all will be saved. Not all will be convinced. No revival in history—beginning at Pentecost—resulted in every person being saved.

I preached a sermon at Westminster Chapel following the horrific event of September 11, 2001. I called it "The Day the World Changed." My book with the same title followed within a month. In it I said that things would eventually get better and better as well as worse and worse; that is, better and better because of the unveiling of the glory of God in the church, but worse and worse when it comes to the display of evil and sin in the world.

Some people thought it was premature to assert that "9/11" (as it is called) was the day the world changed. But it was. I don't think anybody disputes this now. The exponential escalation of violence in the Middle East today—with the ever-increasing spread of terror in the name of religion—can be traced to the Islamic terrorists taking over the airplanes and flying into the twin towers in New York City, the Pentagon, and a field in Pennsylvania, resulting in more than three thousand deaths. And yet the coming Cry as described in Matthew 25:6 will change the world in a much, much greater way.

The good news, then, is that the greatest manifestations of the Holy Spirit in the history of the church—more dramatic than witnessed in any previous awakening or event in history—are at hand. Yes, the impact of the coming Midnight Cry throughout the world will far, far exceed what happened in America on September 11, 2001.

Readers of *Holy Fire* will recall my view that there has been a silent divorce in the church, generally speaking, between the Word and the Spirit. When there is a divorce, sometimes the children stay with the mother, sometimes with the father. In the divorce between the Word and the Spirit you have those on the Word side and those on the Spirit side.

Those on the Word side emphasize earnestly contending for the faith once delivered to the saints, sound teaching, expository preaching, and a return to rediscovery of justification by faith and the sovereignty of God (as taught by Martin Luther, John Calvin, and Jonathan Edwards). What is wrong with that emphasis? Nothing. It is exactly right.

Those on the Spirit side believe that the honor of God's name will not be restored until we get back to the Book of Acts where there were signs, wonders, and miracles—gifts of the Spirit in operation—and where prayer meetings resulted in places being shaken. If you got into Peter's shadow, you were healed; if you lied to the Holy Spirit, you were struck dead. What is wrong with this emphasis? Nothing. It is exactly right. The problem is, it seems to be one or the other—throughout much of the world.

When the Word and Spirit come together at an optimum level—as in Acts 2—the simultaneous combination will result in spontaneous combustion. It is my view that the Midnight Cry of Matthew 25:6 will result in the *ultimate* coming together of the Word and Spirit as seen initially in the Book of Acts. This is when authentic apostolic power in preaching the gospel will be restored to the church before the second coming of Jesus Christ.

The major purpose of this book is to give the reader a mini wake-up call before *the final* wake-up call—the Midnight Cry—comes. As we will see later, it will be too late for the foolish virgins to repent after the Midnight Cry comes. But it is not too late now.

PART 1
PROPHETIC ANALOGY

CHAPTER 1

ISHMAEL

You shall call his name Ishmael.
—GENESIS 16:11

Abraham said to God, "Oh, that Ishmael might live before You!"
—GENESIS 17:18

ISHMAEL IS MY NAME FOR THE PENTECOSTAL AND CHARISMATIC movements. Isaac is my name for the coming move of God on the earth. In the Preface I explained that this book is an extension of the chapter called "Isaac" in my book *Holy Fire*. In fact, I might have called this very book *Isaac*.

The purpose of this chapter is to achieve two things: first, to outline the biblical background of Ishmael in the Old Testament; second, to show that the Pentecostal and Charismatic movements are an essential part of God's strategy in the world. These movements are precursors to the greatest move of the Holy Spirit in the history of the church. Many Pentecostals and Charismatics had assumed that their movements represent God's ultimate blessing of the Spirit before the end. But I shall show that just as Abraham sincerely and understandably believed that Ishmael was the promised child, so these movements understandably believed that they are God's final plan before the second coming. To Abraham's astonishment and disappointment he learned—and finally accepted—that Ishmael was not God's promised child after all; Isaac was coming.

Some Pentecostals and Charismatics might be offended by this analogy. I hope that by explaining my idea of who Ishmael is later in this book, I will alleviate their concerns, but I do truly understand their reaction. There is a natural thrill to being part of what God has been doing—and assuming that no greater movement will be coming down the road. After all, the exponential growth of these movements is enough to make any of those involved to assume they are a part of God's ultimate plan prior to the second coming. Then to learn that something greater is coming gives one a slight feeling of hurt or disappointment. That was precisely Abraham's reaction. It takes a bit of humility to climb down and accept what God has in mind, especially when it does not fit with our hopes and dreams.

I will never forget asking a Charismatic leader in Britain a question: Is the Charismatic movement Ishmael or Isaac?

He replied, "Isaac."

I said to him, "What if I told you that the Charismatic movement is Ishmael?"

He replied, "I hope not."

His reaction was very like that of Abraham who naturally wanted Ishmael to be the promised son. The news of Isaac coming did not bless Abraham—at first. But just as Abraham adjusted to the news about Isaac, I have been encouraged to see how many Charismatics are now responding positively to my analogy. They are saying, "We hope you are right. We need more than what we have at the moment."

Ishmael is the name God gave to Abraham's firstborn son (Gen. 16:11). Sarah, Abraham's wife, was not the mother; Hagar, Sarah's maidservant, gave birth to Ishmael. Abraham had always assumed that his wife Sarah would be the mother of the son that was promised to him. But Sarah—and also Abraham—eventually lost heart that she would ever bear a child. She fully believed that God promised Abraham he would have a son. Believing that promise to her fingertips, Sarah persuaded Abraham to sleep with Hagar. After all, if a male child was born, who is to say that is not what God had in mind all along? So Ishmael was born, and for the next thirteen years Abraham assumed that Ishmael was the promised child that God had in mind.

Here is the background. In Genesis 15 we find a wealthy but discouraged Abraham. He and Sarah were both elderly and without children. He said to God in so many words, "You have given me no children. This means that a servant in my household will be my heir." Wrong.

God said to Abraham, "A son coming from *your own body* will be your heir." God continued, "Count the stars...so shall your offspring be."

Abraham might have said, "Don't joke with me. Don't tease me. Do you really expect me to believe that I in my eighties and Sarah in her seventies would have a son?"

Many of us might have responded like that.

But that was not Abraham's reaction. He actually *believed* the Lord! As a consequence of Abraham believing the Lord, God *credited* Abraham's faith as "righteousness" (vv. 2–6).

This account became Paul's chief illustration for his teaching of justification by faith alone (Rom. 4:1–5; Gal. 3:6–9). Believing that Jesus's death on the cross atones for our sins—and assures us of eternal life—would be as hard to believe as Abraham believing he would be the father of many nations!

But those who believe this gospel are promised forgiveness of sins and a home in heaven! In other words, those who believe the gospel get righteousness *imputed* to them! That means righteousness put to our credit as though we had produced it ourselves. *Imputed* means "put to the credit of."

That is what ultimately matters: the way God sees us. *Our faith counts for righteousness.* That is what Romans 4 is largely about. It all begins with God's promise to Abraham in Genesis 15:6, namely, that Abraham believed the Lord and his faith counted for righteousness. This is the very foundation of the true gospel of Jesus Christ.

However, months and months rolled on without Sarah getting pregnant. At the approximate age of seventy-five Sarah suggested to Abraham—aged around eighty-six—that he might sleep with Hagar, her maidservant. This was not seen as anything immoral in those days. "It may be that I will obtain children through her," Sarah reasoned (Gen. 16:2).

Abraham took her advice. Ishmael was born. Therefore for the next thirteen years Abraham took it for granted that Ishmael was truly the promised son whom God must have had in mind all along. Very understandable. After all, Ishmael was a male child from Abraham's body.

For a good while many Pentecostals and Charismatics have

understandably believed that they represented the ultimate promise of what God had in mind all along before Jesus's second coming. It has been called everything from "last days ministries" to "latter rain" to "the latter day glory of the church." Whatever label given to it, why need anyone look further than what God has obviously accomplished in recent years?

But one day God surprised Abraham with news that was not all that pleasant to him—at least at first: *Sarah will conceive. Isaac is coming.* This meant that the promise God gave to Abraham (Gen. 15:2–6) moreover would refer to *Isaac* not Ishmael.

This news did not thrill Abraham. "Oh, that Ishmael might live before You!" (Gen. 17:18). The New International Version says, "If only Ishmael might live under your blessing!"

Abraham had become very attached to Ishmael. His life had been bound up with Ishmael. He had come to terms with the thought that Hagar's son was whom God had in mind regarding the promise of a son in Genesis 15:6. The news that Sarah would conceive and that Isaac was coming was not what Abraham expected or wanted to hear.

The British Charismatic leader to whom I referred earlier was disappointed at the thought that the great movement of which he was a part might not be God's final promise to the world before the second coming. He wanted to believe that the Charismatic movement of which he was a part was "it." Surely the Pentecostal/Charismatic movement was the ultimate plan of God. After all, has not the Pentecostal/Charismatic movement been an incredible work of God all over the world? The very thought that something *greater* than this movement in the future could be on God's agenda was somehow threatening to him.

But I understood how he felt.

The bottom line of this book is that the greatest move of the Holy Spirit *ever* is coming, surpassing anything in church history since Pentecost. What we have seen in the twentieth century—the rise of the Pentecostal movement in 1906 and the Charismatic movement in 1960, great though these movements have been—is *Ishmael.*

But *Isaac is coming.*

This is a message I had preached a number of times at Westminster

Chapel from my earliest days there. In fact, when I invited Arthur Blessitt to preach for us in 1982, one person who knew of my position on this wrote and asked, "Why are you having Ishmael [viz. Arthur] to preach for you?" They knew I was waiting for Isaac and thought I had compromised by having Ishmael!

I remember discussing this idea of Ishmael and Isaac with Dr. Martyn Lloyd-Jones—that the Charismatic movement is like Ishmael, but the next great move of God will be Isaac. Dr. Lloyd-Jones had preached the previous weekend for a Charismatic "celebration," as they called it. It was the first and only time he preached for Charismatics. He told me how much he enjoyed it. He looked at me and said, "I kept thinking of you the whole time. I wondered if you have come into the kingdom for such a time as this." I will never forget him telling me that as long as I live.

If you regard yourself as either a Pentecostal or a Charismatic, I sincerely hope you will not be offended by my analogy. It should not be seen as a put-down of this movement. Quite the opposite. After all, I call myself a Reformed Charismatic. Second, not every detail of the original story of Abraham, Sarah, and Hagar would apply to the Pentecostal/Charismatic movement. Even a parable often does not "stand on all four legs." Therefore one should not try to make all the details of the original account apply in a particular manner to Pentecostals and Charismatics. The big point is: as the promise concerning Isaac was a hundred times greater than the promise concerning Ishmael, so too will the next great move of God be infinitely greater than anything we know about in church history.

Third, these things said, I do wonder if there is not a parallel between Abraham listening to Sarah—in order to make good God's promise—and some Charismatics today who sometimes try to make things happen. Have we not seen this sort of thing take place in our day, namely, people trying to make some promises of God "fit"? It is my own view that the greatest weakness of some Charismatics today is their trying to *make things happen*. Whether it be a healing or a miracle, so often some have a need to prove themselves—that God has done something. The truth is, the greatest freedom is having nothing to prove. I fear that the greatest weakness among many Charismatics is trying to force God to act when God may not *choose* to act. And if I am totally vulnerable, it seems to me that the greatest theological weakness in the Pentecostal/Charismatic movement is the apparent lack of faith that *some* seem to have in the sovereignty of God. A robust view of the sovereignty of God, however, could result in their *stopping* to force God's hand to "do things."

Fourth, let no one think I am comparing Charismatics to Muslims when I call Charismatics by the nickname Ishmael. Such a comparison never crossed my mind.

But what *has* crossed my mind is that God has given a promise to the seed of Ishmael—virtually the entire Arab world. As God gave a *huge* promise concerning Ishmael—one which should never be underestimated, I predict that millions of Muslims will be converted virtually overnight. This will be part of the consequence of the Midnight Cry. Furthermore, there are many Muslims in non-Arabic countries—such as Indonesia, Malaysia, and Bangladesh. The coming revival will have a major impact on all Muslim countries throughout the world.

FAITH, NOT UNBELIEF, LED TO THE BIRTH OF ISHMAEL

The truth is, what Abraham and Sarah agreed upon was not rooted in unbelief but faith. It is *because* of their faith in the reliability of God's promise to Abraham that they proceeded as they did. Had Sarah doubted God's word to Abraham, she would not have made the suggestion she did, nor would Abraham have acquiesced had he doubted God's word.

Never forget, then, that Sarah's suggestion that Abraham sleep with Hagar was motivated out of a persuasion that God *truly did promise Abraham a son.* She was therefore not acting in unbelief; quite the opposite. She was acting in faith. Moreover, Sarah initially acted out of unselfishness. Can you imagine how much she must have wanted to have a child of her own? She very likely blamed herself that she could not have children. Furthermore, Abraham almost certainly accepted her suggestion out of a willingness to do what it takes to help God's promise along. Abraham is not to be blamed for listening to Sarah. He may have felt that he was being irresponsible not to exhaust every possibility to make good God's promise to him since the years were rolling by without any evidence that God was at work.

Abraham no doubt gave into Sarah's suggestion because he lost hope that she could get pregnant. Had there been no Hagar, yes, Sarah would have given birth to a son later. Sleeping with Hagar, at any rate, was Sarah's idea. Abraham sleeping with Hagar was not only honoring Sarah's advice but was done *only* because he believed God's word to him. Surely a male child would legitimize Abraham's decision to sleep with Hagar, this being the way he no doubt reasoned. Can he be faulted for this? In a word: Abraham acted upon the principle of faith.

Abraham therefore slept with Hagar. She conceived. But when it was obvious that Hagar was pregnant, Sarah did not cope so well. She did not calculate that Hagar having her husband's child would be so upsetting. A severe quarrel between Abraham and Sarah emerged with Sarah blaming Abraham for her suffering. Sarah felt despised by Hagar. Sarah began to mistreat Hagar, and Hagar fled.

The angel of the Lord came to Hagar in the desert. She explained to the angel that she was running from Sarah. God through the angel immediately commanded Hagar, "Return to your mistress, and submit yourself to her authority," adding, "I will multiply your descendants exceedingly so that they will be too many to count." God also stated to Hagar, "You are pregnant and will bear a son. You shall call his name Ishmael, because the LORD has heard your affliction" (Gen. 16:9–11).

Hagar was almost overwhelmed with a feeling of God's love—that God would even notice her. "Then she called the name of the LORD that spoke to her, 'You are the God who sees,' for she said, 'Have I now looked on Him who sees me?'" (v. 13). I love the King James Version: "Thou God seest me."

It was a moving moment—when God Himself affirmed Hagar and she submitted to God. Hagar's experience with God in the desert must not be forgotten or underestimated. God was showing that He was behind what was happening. The name *Ishmael* means "God hears."

Ishmael was not merely Sarah's idea; he was *God's* idea.

The Pentecostal Movement
Was Born in Faith

The Pentecostal/Charismatic movement can be traced to the famed Azusa Street Revival that lasted at least three years from 1906 to 1909. The central figure was William Seymour (1870–1922), an African American and son of former slaves in Louisiana. He was converted in a Methodist church in Indiana, then became affiliated with the Church of God of Anderson, Indiana. After that he studied at God's Bible School in Cincinnati, Ohio, led by Martin Wells Knapp, a holiness leader who taught two works of grace—being "saved" and then "sanctified." Seymour moved to Houston, Texas, where he came under the influence of Charles Fox Parham—his chief mentor—who taught that speaking in tongues is the evidence of the baptism of the Holy Spirit.

In 1906 Seymour moved to Los Angeles, California. A soft-spoken teacher, not known as an orator, Seymour began holding meetings in a run-down mission under the name of "Apostolic Faith." People of different races attended. It was said that "the color line was washed away in the blood."[1]

The Holy Spirit fell on these meetings in an amazing manner. People spoke in tongues, many were healed, some fell to the floor spontaneously, and many were reportedly delivered of demons. Word spread all over the area, which resulted in hundreds coming to see what was happening. They began holding three services a day seven days a week for three years, these being known later as the "the glory days." Noted historian Vinson Synan in *An Eyewitness Remembers the Century of the Holy Spirit* (Chosen Books) observed that "while it seemed unlikely at the time, the Azusa Street Revival would serve as a major turning point in world Christian history."[2]

The Pentecostal movement was born in spontaneous revival—"outside the camp" (Heb. 13:13). Both the secular press and the historic denominations (e.g., Methodist, Baptist, Episcopal, and Presbyterian) tried to take little notice of the Azusa Street Revival or its growth. The *Los Angeles Daily Times* called the worshippers "a new sect of fanatics."[3] This article was published on the same day that the great earthquake happened in San Francisco.

People began coming from all over America and all over the world to see what was going on in Los Angeles. It is alleged that one of these was the Englishman Smith Wigglesworth (1859–1947), who became a prominent healing evangelist in the United Kingdom. Although the Welsh Revival (1904–1905) was not known for people speaking in tongues, the Jeffreys brothers—George and Stephen—were converted in the Welsh Revival. George Jeffreys founded the Elim Pentecostal Church in Great Britain, and Stephen was a leading figure in the Assemblies of God in Britain.[4]

I have read several accounts of the Azusa Street Revival. I have also talked with some who have researched it thoroughly. The Azusa Street Revival was truly amazing. I don't mean to be unfair, but surely only those with deep prejudice toward the immediate witness of the Holy Spirit would be unmoved by the true accounts of what happened. Please read the aforementioned book by Vinson Synan and also his *Holiness Pentecostal Tradition*. I suspect too that racial prejudice was partly at the bottom of some people's negative attitude toward the origin of modern Pentecostalism since the principle figure, William Seymour, was black. The meetings were interracial, which was very unusual at that time. Speaking in tongues became synonymous with the name Pentecostal. Indeed, Pentecostalism became such a stigma that the early Nazarenes voted to change their name from Pentecostal Church of the Nazarene to Church of the Nazarene.

The immediate heirs of the Azusa Street Revival were Pentecostal denominations that sprung up—for example, Pentecostal Holiness, International Church of the Foursquare Gospel, Assemblies of God, Church of God in Christ, and the Church of God of Cleveland, Tennessee. In the late 1940s there emerged a new phenomenon—healing revivals. The leading evangelist was Oral Roberts (1918–2009), a member of the Pentecostal Holiness church.

THE RISE OF THE CHARISMATIC MOVEMENT

However, in 1960 a movement initially called Glossolalia (from the Gr. *glossa*—tongue) sprang up in America. It penetrated the old-line denominations, this apparently being the first time speaking in tongues was witnessed outside the historic Pentecostal churches. It eventually became known as the Charismatic movement. At Easter 1960 Dennis Bennett, rector of St. Mark's Episcopal Church in Van Nuys, California, revealed to his parish that he had a Pentecostal experience—speaking in tongues. He was eventually forced out of his church but was offered St. Luke's Episcopal Church in Seattle, Washington, where he was allowed to continue his ministry. The officials there figured they had nothing to lose since St. Luke's was virtually empty in any case. Within a year the congregation increased to nearly a thousand. Our dear friends to whom my book *It Ain't Over Till It's Over* is dedicated, Bill and Vivian Burnett, sat under Dennis Bennett's ministry in those days. They took their family and friends to the Friday night "baptism in the Holy Spirit meetings."

Also in the 1960s, largely through the influence of South African minister David du Plessis (1905–1987), speaking in tongues spread to nearly every major denomination in America—including Catholicism—and spread right around the world. As the Christian faith spread to the third world, among the primary carriers were those who had the Pentecostal experience. The latest statistics indicate that the Pentecostal/Charismatic movement numbers at least 610 million.[5] Most of this began in the Azusa Street Mission in Los Angeles in 1906.

The principle reason I call this great movement Ishmael is that—although it has been a wonderful blessing to the world—it is not *the final plan of God* for the church and the world. It is because of my conviction that something greater than what we have at the moment is desperately needed.

In addition to this is our previously mentioned view that there has been a silent divorce in the church, generally speaking, between the Word and the Spirit. I believe the two must come together before the world is to be shaken afresh. Something huge needs to happen, but thankfully something greater than ever *is* coming. If you ask what will the convergence of the Word and Spirit as I envisage in this book look like, I reply: it will be as it was on the Day of Pentecost: (1) the preaching of the gospel with virtually irresistible power; (2) many conversions; (3) a restoration of the fear of God; and (4) signs and wonders (Acts 2:1–43).

The Ishmael-Isaac analogy is our concept that came out of this conviction. I have wanted to show in this chapter that the Pentecostal/ Charismatic movement has been sovereignly and strategically raised up by God but that this is not the final move of the Holy Spirit before the second coming.

CHAPTER 2

ISAAC

Abraham called the name of his son...whom Sarah bore to him, Isaac.
—**GENESIS 21:3**

But at midnight there was a cry, "Look, the
bridegroom is coming! Come out to meet him!"
—**MATTHEW 25:6**

ABRAHAM WAS DEVOTED TO ISHMAEL. ABRAHAM HAD BECOME convinced that Ishmael was the promised child. The last thing he expected at the age of one hundred—with Sarah being ninety—was the word of the Lord that came to him about Sarah: "I will bless her and also give you a son by her. I will bless her, and she will be the mother of nations. Kings of peoples will come from her" (Gen. 17:16). Indeed, "I will establish My covenant with Isaac" (v. 21). In other words: Isaac is coming and Ishmael is not the promised child after all. It was almost as though God said to Abraham, "Sorry, Abraham, like it or not, Isaac is coming."

Abraham was not happy with the news that the covenant would be established through Isaac. "Oh, that Ishmael might live before You!" (v. 18). As I said earlier, many Charismatics understandably want to feel that their movement—which has had prodigious success all over the world—is *the* final statement of God regarding what to expect before the second coming. However, I believe the next great movement of the Holy Spirit will exceed, transcend, and virtually eclipse all previous movements of God by comparison.

As I mentioned previously, the promise concerning Isaac was a hundred times greater than the promise concerning Ishmael. I believe that the next great move of God on the earth—beginning with the Midnight

Cry—will be a hundred times greater than the impact of the Pentecostal/ Charismatic movement.

AN APPEAL TO CHARISMATICS AND REFORMED

Abraham loved Ishmael so much that he pleaded with God for the promise of his seed to be given to Ishmael not Isaac. Abraham is the father of us all. Abraham loved Ishmael but accepted Isaac. I appeal now to Pentecostals, Charismatics, Reformed, and all Evangelicals. I appeal to those who love the Word and want to see a restoration of the pure gospel. I appeal to those who are open to the immediate and direct witness of the Holy Spirit. Let us attempt to overthrow our prejudices that keep us from appreciating what God has done in history that may be outside our comfort zones.

SMITH WIGGLESWORTH'S REPORTED PROPHECY

Some readers will know about the alleged prophecy of Smith Wigglesworth (1859–1947), which he reportedly gave shortly before he died in 1947. He was part of the Pentecostal movement in England years before the emergence of the Charismatic movement that came in around 1960, crossing all denominational barriers. He had an amazing global ministry, stretching all over Europe and also to New Zealand. He is better known for his healing gift than his prophetic gift. I have read several eyewitness accounts of his extraordinary healing ministry inside and outside England, especially Switzerland and Sweden. That said, he is the first to forecast the emergence of what is now called the Charismatic movement and also the first to prophesy the coming together of the Word and Spirit, which he claimed would result in the greatest revival of all time. He is alleged to have prophesied the house church movement in the UK that came in the 1970s. The reported prophecy of 1947 was put on the Internet in 1997:

> During the next few decades there will be two distinct moves of the Holy Spirit across the church in Great Britain. The first move will affect every church that is open to receive it and will be characterized by a restoration of the baptism and gifts of the Holy Spirit.

The second move of the Holy Spirit will result in people leaving historic churches and planting new churches. In the duration of each of these moves, the people who are involved will say, "This is the great revival." But the Lord says "No, neither is this the great revival but both are steps towards it."

When the new church phase is on the wane, there will be evidenced in the churches something that has not been seen before: a coming together of those with an emphasis on the Word and those with an emphasis on the Spirit.

When the Word and the Spirit come together, there will be the biggest movement of the Holy Spirit that the nation, and indeed the world, has ever seen. It will mark the beginning of a revival that will eclipse anything that has been witnessed within these shores, even the Wesleyan and the Welsh revivals of former years. The outpouring of God's Spirit will flow over from the UK to the mainland of Europe, and from there will begin a missionary move to the ends of the earth.[1]

I had not heard of this prophecy when I predicted virtually the same thing at our first Word and Spirit Conference in 1992. Funnily enough, several people thought I got it from Wigglesworth. George Stormont, Wigglesworth's friend and biographer, was evidently the first to put it in print. But what appears on the Internet is an embellishment of what Stormont attributed to Wigglesworth in the biography.

According to Stormont, Wigglesworth prophesied two moves of the Spirit: (1) a restoration of the gifts of the Spirit (i.e., what we would call the Charismatic movement) and (2) a coming together of the Word and Spirit (i.e., what I have chosen to call Isaac). Wigglesworth said that when the Word and Spirit combine, "We shall see the greatest move the church of Jesus Christ has ever seen."[2] And yet the latter is the only point I made in the first place. Frankly I don't need Wigglesworth's alleged prophecy to convince me, but there is no doubt in my mind that he said virtually the same thing many years before I said it.

I believe that the greatest move of God on the earth since Pentecost—when the Word and Spirit come together at optimum level—is the next thing to take place on God's calendar. It is when the Word and Spirit will coalesce and the entire church will be shaken rigid. The church that turned the world upside down in the days of the early church will be turned upside down again.

Isaac, then, is the name I have given to the convergence of the Word and Spirit—the event that will lead to the next great and final move of God on the earth.

There are at least two ways of perceiving Isaac, assuming you might be generally sympathetic with this metaphor. One is to welcome the next great move of the Holy Spirit on the earth but keep it separate from eschatology. In other words, there are some who may like my idea of the next move of God being the coming together of the Word and the Spirit and the emphasis on Romans 4; they simply do not think it has anything to do with end times or a movement just prior to the second coming. This would mean that the next great move of God would merely be in the tradition of the New England Great Awakening, the Wesleyan Revival, the Cane Ridge Revival, the Welsh Revival, and so forth. Therefore the next great move of God in this case would not be the *last* great move of God.

I welcome those who would take this view. We all surely agree that a fresh outpouring of the Holy Spirit is needed—whatever name you want to give it. We are all on the same team when it comes to agreeing on this. You certainly don't have to agree with all the details I present in this book.

However, it is my view that the next great move of God on the earth is indeed *eschatological*. I am convinced we are in the very last days. The final great move of God on the earth is propounded throughout the Bible, namely, a day when the "earth will be filled with the knowledge of the glory of the LORD, as the waters cover the seas" (Hab. 2:14).

Granted, there are many scholars and Bible students who agree that a fulfillment of this prophecy will precede the second coming. They are merely loath to say that it is coming any time *soon*! Quite understandably, they don't want to be like those who felt that what was going on in their own day was "it"! Jonathan Edwards honestly thought that what he saw in his day was "it." Could you blame him? So could I be wrong too? Of course I could.

But I am saying that the Midnight Cry will lead to the final, great move of the Holy Spirit on the earth and is coming soon. The Word and Spirit will come together at an optimum level as in the Book of Acts. Many have thought that the Charismatic movement is God's last move before the end. I can understand why they feel this way. But no. There is much, much more to come. At the same time many Evangelicals assume that their own particular understanding of the Word is all that is necessary to believe as we wait for the second coming. I wish it were not so, but there is minimal expectancy among many Evangelicals that a great outpouring of the Spirit will come prior to the second coming. Thus not many on either side of the spectrum have been persuaded that there is more to come.

One difference between Ishmael and Isaac—at the moment—is that Ishmael is still alive and well, as it were: flourishing in many parts of the world, but struggling in many parts of the world too. Isaac, however, is still future; the Midnight Cry has not come yet. As I said, I have had a number of Charismatics and Pentecostals who are very sympathetic with my analogy who say to me, "We hope you are right. If what we have at the moment is all there is, we are in pretty bad shape." Moreover, many in Pentecostal churches, house churches, and those Charismatics in denominational churches have become aware that "the fire has gone out; we need something."

I offer hope in this book—not merely because I am trying to be encouraging; it is because Isaac *is* coming. This has been a conviction of mine I have held on to for many, many years. That in itself proves nothing of course. But I would go to the stake for this. I have thought it would come in my lifetime because of a vision I had in 1956. If this does not come in my lifetime—as I hope for, it will come. It is not far away.

This will be a movement of the Spirit that will exceed our greatest expectations. I won't be pompous and say, "This prophetic analogy is from the Lord"; that claim would go against all I teach about making statements like that. Such claiming is dealt with in my book *Pigeon Religion: Holy Spirit Is That You?* I will leave it to the reader to decide whether the insight makes sense to you.

In a word: Ishmael—the Pentecostal/Charismatic movement—is an essential part of God's plan. But the best is yet to come—Isaac. Such a promise took Abraham by surprise. It took Sarah by surprise. I think it will take virtually all of us by surprise. Both Abraham and Sarah laughed at the very idea that Isaac would come at their age. It seemed utterly far-fetched. But they soon stopped laughing and started believing. It is my prayer that you will be gripped by what you read in this book, that the Holy Spirit will convict you that the best is yet to be—this being before the physical return of our Lord to the earth.

PART 2
THE PARABLE OF
THE TEN VIRGINS

CHAPTER 3

INTRODUCING THE PARABLE OF THE TEN VIRGINS

Then the kingdom of heaven shall be like ten virgins, who
took their lamps and went out to meet the bridegroom.
—MATTHEW 25:1

Your word is a lamp to my feet.
—PSALM 119:105

Then Samuel took the horn of oil, and anointed him
in the midst of his brothers. And the Spirit of the
LORD came on David from that day forward.
—1 SAMUEL 16:13

Shorthand to Understand the Parable of the Ten Virgins

- The Bridegroom = Jesus
- The ten virgins = part of the church generally
- Wise virgins = Christians who pursue the Word and the Spirit
- Foolish virgins = Christians who do not pursue the Word and Spirit
- Lamp = Word
- Oil = Spirit
- Asleep = spiritual condition of the church in the last days
- Midnight = middle of the night when the church is in a deep sleep
- Midnight Cry = wake-up call to the church that Jesus is coming soon
- Messengers (implied) = Christians who cry out in the middle of the night
- All virgins waking up = the church waking up
- Coming of the Bridegroom = the second coming (first spiritual, then physical)
- Wedding banquet = celebration of the bride making herself ready
- Shut door = when it is too late for repentance

As you read this chapter I ask you: Are you a wise virgin? Or are you a foolish virgin?

It is my prayer that this book will serve to keep you from being a foolish virgin. If this book makes you believe you are a foolish virgin, good! That means you are getting a wake-up call now. There is time to change. You can cross over immediately and become—and remain—a wise virgin.

But when the Midnight Cry comes, it will be too late for the foolish virgins to become wise virgins. This does not mean that the foolish virgins go to hell and are eternally lost. It means they forfeit their inheritance. This means they will not be allowed to enjoy the wedding banquet—the great revival. People like this will be a very miserable lot. As I said, I want this book to serve as a mini wake-up call to the reader lest they be found out when it is too late. It is not too late now.

There are *three* categories of Christians in the parable of the ten virgins: (1) the wise virgins; (2) the foolish virgins; and (3) the messengers, those who are *not* asleep but are the ones who are used to wake up the church in the last days. They are the ones who *announce* that the second coming of Jesus is at hand—and the church is awakened. The parable focuses on the wise and foolish virgins that typify the church, generally speaking; but there is a third category of people, namely, those who are God's instruments to wake up the church.

The parable of the ten virgins is introduced in Matthew 25:1 by the words "at that time" (NIV) or "then" (MEV). This is because the Midnight Cry will come when it is not expected. The parable begins right after Jesus gave His final application of the eschatological Mount Olivet discourse in Matthew 24. Having warned His hearers to be ready at all times, Jesus illustrates His point with the short story of the "owner of the house" being taken surprise by a thief (Matt. 24:43–44), followed by the easily overlooked parable of the unfaithful servant who is not ready for his master's return (vv. 45–51). But Jesus is not finished because Matthew 25 starts with, "*At that time* the kingdom of heaven will be like ten virgins" (NIV, emphasis added).

I therefore see the parable of the ten virgins as eschatological (referring to the last days) and prophetic (referring to the spiritual condition of the church). It includes Jesus's prophetic implication that the church will be *asleep* in the very last days.

THE WORD AND SPIRIT

We have the Word and Spirit in this parable. The lamp refers to the Word. "Your word is a lamp to my feet and a light to my path" (Ps. 119:105). The oil refers to the Spirit. When Samuel took the horn of oil and anointed the next king, "the Spirit of the LORD" came upon young David (1 Sam. 16:13).

The wise virgins in Matthew 25 are those who not only had the Word but also pursued the Spirit; they kept their lamps burning by taking sufficient oil. They "took jars of oil with their lamps" (v. 4). The foolish, however, had the Word but "took no oil with them" (v. 3). And yet their lamps were burning *at first*, showing they were regenerate. They said later that their lamps had "gone out" (v. 8). They simply did not take enough oil to keep their lamps burning. They were saved—but only just.

Inheritance

Does this mean that people like this lose their salvation? No. But they do lose their inheritance. Inheritance is manifested two ways: internal (your walk with Christ) and external (your calling in life). The way this works out in the parable of the ten virgins is this: the wise virgins' inheritance is to enjoy the wedding banquet and then receive a reward at the judgment seat of Christ. Because the foolish virgins forfeited their inheritance, they are shut out of the wedding banquet and receive no reward at the judgment seat of Christ. Paul says they are saved by fire (1 Cor. 3:15).

All Christians are called to come into their inheritance; some do, some don't.

Inheritance is God's reward to those who persist in faith. The Lord chose our inheritance for us (Ps. 47:4). David, an obedient servant of God, could say, "The lines have fallen for me in pleasant places; yes, an inheritance is beautiful for me" (Ps. 16:6). We should all be able to say that. But not all Christians are equally obedient.

The word *inheritance* can be used interchangeably with reward, prize, or crown:

> Do you not know that all those who run in a race run, but one receives the prize? So run, that you may obtain it. Everyone who strives for the prize exercises self-control in all things. Now they do it to obtain a corruptible crown, but we an incorruptible one. So, therefore, I run, not with uncertainty. So I fight, not as one who beats the air. But I bring and keep my body under subjection, lest when preaching to others I myself should be disqualified.
> —1 Corinthians 9:24–27

> Knowing that from the Lord you will receive the reward of the inheritance.
> —Colossians 3:24

> I have fought a good fight, I have finished my course, and I have kept the faith. From now on a crown of righteousness is laid up for me, which the Lord, the righteous Judge, will give me on that Day, and not only to me but also to all who have loved His appearing.
> —2 Timothy 4:7–8

Not being rejected for the prize was very important to the apostle Paul. It was sadly not important to the foolish virgins who did not take oil in their lamps. I pray that wanting the prize or crown will be very important to all readers of this book.

Salvation and inheritance are not the same thing; salvation is one thing, inheritance another. For example:

- Salvation refers to being saved from God's wrath. Inheritance is the reward for persistent faith.

- Saving faith gets you to heaven; persistent faith gets you your inheritance on earth.

- Salvation means we will go to heaven when we die. Inheritance means a reward at the judgment seat of Christ.

In the parable of the ten virgins the inheritance of the wise virgins is that they are invited into the wedding banquet. If you and I are like the wise virgins, then we will be invited to enjoy the greatest move of the Holy Spirit since Pentecost.

Isaac is coming. Isaac is coming soon.

Being *saved* is what makes a Christian a Christian. There are terms that are synonymous with salvation: being regenerated—born again; being redeemed—bought by Christ's blood; being justified—when righteousness is put to our credit. Receiving an inheritance, however, is God's reward for Christians who persist in their faith. This reward is internal and external. The internal reward is coming to rest in God; it is full assurance of faith. The external inheritance is experiencing what God has called you to do—whether a teacher, nurse, or professional person. All of us may have virtually the same *internal* inheritance, but not all have the same external inheritance.

TWO KINDS OF FAITH

There are therefore basically two kinds of faith: saving faith and persistent faith. Saving faith, also called justifying faith, is what makes you fit for heaven because Christ's righteousness is put to your credit. Persistent faith, however, is what gets you your inheritance because you were obedient. Examples of inheritance by persistent faith are in Hebrews 11. The faith described in Hebrews 11 is not saving faith; it is a description of those stalwarts who came into their inheritance by not giving up.

Inheritance is that which "accompanies" salvation (Heb. 6:9). But sadly not all who are saved necessarily come into their inheritance. I repeat: All Christians are called to receive an inheritance. Some do; some don't. Those who don't *forfeit* a reward at the judgment seat of Christ.

> For we must all appear before the judgment seat of Christ, that each one may receive his recompense in the body, according to what he has done, whether it was good or bad.
>
> —2 CORINTHIANS 5:10

Those who do not persist in faith "suffer loss" of reward, although they will be saved "by fire" (1 Cor. 3:15, KJV). Those who will lose a reward but are saved by fire are depicted as foolish virgins in the parable of the ten virgins. Those who pursue their inheritance by persistent faith are the wise virgins; they are invited to the wedding banquet. Such people will receive a reward at the judgment seat of Christ. Likewise those Christians who pursue both the Word and Spirit—and are living at the time of the Midnight Cry—will *enjoy* the greatest move of the Spirit since Pentecost. The foolish virgins typify Christians who have a good beginning but do not persistently pursue the Word and the Spirit. They will be extremely sad and sorry when the Midnight Cry comes.

Matthew 25 includes three eschatological parables: the parable of the ten virgins, the parable of the talents, and the parable of the sheep and goats. All three in different ways point to the final judgment.

When I was a teenager, I heard a memorable sermon on the parable of the ten virgins. The minister brought a huge clock to the pulpit with the hands showing that it was five minutes before twelve o'clock midnight. Midnight was interpreted to mean the end of the age—the time when Jesus would return to the earth a second time. He persuaded me that Jesus was coming very soon and that there was little time left. I assumed then that the Midnight Cry meant twelve o'clock midnight and signaled both the end of the age and the exact time of the second coming. But no. It is not that. It means that there will be a cry in the middle of the night, metaphorically speaking—when the church is sound asleep.

THE ANCIENT MIDDLE EASTERN WEDDING

My book *The Parables of Jesus* includes the parable of the ten virgins. As I said above, many of the parables of Jesus do not stand evenly "on all four legs"; you must discover the main point He makes and not try to make every detail fit. That said, some of the parables might justly be interpreted allegorically. I believe the parable of the ten virgins comes into this category, but one must still be cautious and not try too hard to make every detail "fit."

One oddity in this parable is that the bride herself is not mentioned but only implied. The ten virgins are like bridesmaids. And yet at the same time they typify the church. The omission of the bride invites one to interpret the parable in more than one way—and not be wrong in their understanding of Jesus's main point.

It would seem that the parable of the ten virgins is based upon an ancient Middle Eastern wedding. The weddings in those days were much different from ours today. Jesus's immediate hearers might have understood this parable better than we might quickly grasp today. Weddings then took place in the house of the bridegroom. They did not take place in a synagogue or church, in the office of a justice of the peace, or in the registry office.

Sometimes the wedding would take the form of a seven-day celebration. At a specific time the bridegroom would come to take his bride from her house and then take her to his house. The tradition in those days was that there would be young unmarried ladies—bridesmaids— who were friends of the bride and who would accompany the bridal couple from the house of the bride to the house of the groom. The bride would never know exactly when the bridegroom would arrive at her house. Because the exact time of the bridegroom's arrival was uncertain, the bride was expected to be ready to leave at any moment. Often, strange as it may seem to us, the bridegroom would come in the middle of the night!

Jesus's original hearers may have understood this more readily than we do today. I have no way of knowing whether they connected the parable to what Jesus had just taught in Matthew 24, that it would describe the church in the final generation. But Matthew expects you and me to grasp this.

In any case, those unmarried ladies—virgins—who were truly prudent would bring along a flask with additional oil supply so their lamp would be burning in the middle of the night. This way their lamp would always be lit.

Jesus's main point: we should be *ready to rejoice* at the announcement that the Bridegroom's coming is at hand. This is to be a time of celebration, something to enjoy!

But there is no hint that either the wise or foolish virgins rejoiced—at first—when the Cry came. The foolish begged the wise for oil. The wise could only reply they barely had enough for themselves. Sadly this was not a time of rejoicing—but it should have been.

However, once awakened with their lamps trimmed, the wise will be rewarded. They are permitted to be right in the middle of the greatest move of the Holy Spirit since Pentecost. Verses 7–9 in Matthew 25 indicate a measure of time between the sudden Cry and the eventual coming of the Bridegroom:

> Then all those virgins rose and trimmed their lamps. But the foolish said to the wise, "Give us some of your oil, for our lamps have gone out."
>
> The wise answered, "No, lest there not be enough for us and you. Go rather to those who sell it, and buy some for yourselves."

THE GAP IN TIME

It should be clear to you by now that the Midnight Cry and the coming of the Bridegroom are *not simultaneous*. There is a measure of time between the two events, allowing for sufficient time for the conversation that takes place between the foolish and wise virgins. As we will see below, this factor is very important when we examine the immediate fallout of the Midnight Cry.

Owing to the church being asleep, the Midnight Cry will sadly not result immediately in celebration. It will initially precipitate fear—a feeling of awe, of great anxiety. Not unlike the event of September 11, there will be an initial widespread feeling of solemnity. Instead of people generally being thrilled that Jesus is coming soon, it will be characterized by shock. The foolish virgins will realize they do not have oil; the wise virgins will realize they were *just as asleep as the foolish*—and barely had enough oil for themselves.

The parable of the ten virgins is therefore a prophetic parable not only because it is eschatological but also because it forecasts that the church will be in a deep sleep when the Cry finally comes. It is a prophecy that the awakening will come in the middle of the night, metaphorically speaking. In other words, when we are in a deep sleep and not expecting it.

I would add that there is surely no better description of the church today than this; we are asleep. Picture yourself in a deep sleep at 2:00 a.m. when you least expect to be awakened! That is where the church is, spiritually speaking, at the present time.

Two Meanings: Both True

There is yet another characteristic of some of Jesus's parables, namely, they can have more than one valid application. Indeed, some of them have a built-in ambiguity. This purposeful ambiguity lies behind the whole of Matthew 24. Matthew 24 refers to two events: the destruction of Jerusalem and the second coming. As we will see further below, it is not easy to know which verses refer to the destruction of Jerusalem— which took place around AD 67—and the second coming. The best of scholars are divided on this. My point is, there are intended ambiguities in Jesus's teaching and especially some of His parables.

The parable of the ten virgins is certainly such; it refers both to being ready for (1) the physical second coming of Jesus but also to be ready for (2) the Midnight Cry prior to the second coming. This parable is as much about being ready for the Midnight Cry—the ultimate wake-up call—as it is about being ready for Jesus's second coming.

One of the main points of the parable of the ten virgins is that the church *should* be ready for the second coming of Jesus but in fact *won't* be ready for it. According to Jesus, then, *the church will be spiritually asleep* and not watching for Jesus's second coming. The brief parable at the end of Matthew 24 demonstrates the horrific consequences for those not ready for the coming of the Son of man:

> Who then is a faithful and wise servant, whom his master has made ruler over his household to give them food at the appointed time? Blessed is that servant whom his master will find so doing when he comes. Truly, I say to you that he will make him ruler over all his goods. But if that servant says in his heart, "My master delays his coming," and begins to strike his fellow servants and eat and drink with the drunkards, the master of that servant will come on a day when he does not look for him and in an hour he is not aware of

and will cut him in pieces and appoint him his portion with the hypocrites, where there shall be weeping and gnashing of teeth.

—MATTHEW 24:45–51

CHASTENING OR BEING DISCIPLINED

Whereas the Midnight Cry is the ultimate wake-up call, there may be many wake-up calls given to us along the way in the Christian life. For example, chastening is a wake-up call. God may chasten us—discipline us—in a manner that lets us know He is on our case. Those He loves are chastened; it is evidence you are a true child of God. The Lord loves those He disciplines (Heb. 12:6–11).

Keep in mind therefore that we are talking about true Christians. The ten virgins—both wise and foolish—symbolize those who have been born again. Whereas not all who are a part of the professing church are truly regenerate, those in *this* parable are to be seen as saved. First, they are referred to as virgins because the purity of Christ's righteousness has been imputed to them. Second, the fact that the lamps of the foolish virgins had "gone out" shows that oil *was* there. One cannot be converted without the Holy Spirit (John 6:44; Rom. 8:9). They were saved, yes. But only just. So not all saved people are wise; they can be foolish, not pursuing both the Word and the Spirit.

If you are born again, chastening is inevitable. It is only a matter of time until you will experience God's discipline. Sometimes that discipline can be severe. Normally there are three levels of chastening or being disciplined:

1. Plan A—internal, when God speaks to our hearts through His Word. This is clearly the best way to have one's problems solved (Ps. 119:9, 105).

2. Plan B—external chastening, when God resorts to outward means to get our attention—illness, financial reverse, loss, withholding of vindication, and other ways to put us on the right path (Jon. 2:1–5; 1 Cor. 11:30).

3. Plan C—when all the above fail and God intervenes by (a) taking a true Christian home to heaven prematurely

(1 Cor. 11:29–32; 1 John 5:16) or (b) letting one live on but without being able to be restored again to repentance (Heb. 6:4–6).

The foolish virgins are like those who would not be granted repentance. They will be truly sorry, yes—extremely regretful indeed; but it will be too late for them to become wise. As we will see further below, one of the saddest features of the parable of the ten virgins is that no destinies were changed as a result of the Midnight Cry. The wise stayed wise; the foolish virgins remained foolish. There was no crossover from being foolish to becoming wise.

That is one of the reasons for this book! I am hoping to save you from becoming a foolish virgin.

TWO GREAT AWAKENINGS IN AMERICAN CHURCH HISTORY

The Midnight Cry will be a severe and terrifying kind of chastening. A hint of what this might be like took place at least twice in American church history. The first was witnessed in the fallout of Jonathan Edwards's historic sermon "Sinners in the Hands of an Angry God," preached on July 8, 1741, in Enfield, Connecticut. Taking his text from Deuteronomy 32:35—"Their foot shall slide in due time" (KJV), Edwards's sermon on eternal punishment in hell was followed by people holding on to church pews in the building and tree trunks outside—to keep from sliding into hell; such was the effect. It only happened once, although Edwards repeated the sermon later—with no effect at all. It is my view that God did it *once* to give people a hint of the seriousness and awfulness of His wrath toward sin.

The second event took place in Bourbon County, Kentucky, in 1801. It was as though the final judgment were brought forward for a moment. This was the most memorable moment of the Cane Ridge Revival, called America's second Great Awakening. It marked the beginning of the era of camp meetings. On a Sunday morning—August 9, 1801—standing on a fallen tree, a Methodist lay preacher took his text from 2 Corinthians 5:10, "For we must all appear before the judgment seat of Christ; that every one may receive the things done in his body, according to that he hath done, whether it be good or bad" (KJV). An estimated fifteen thousand people heard the sermon.

As he spoke on the final judgment, the fear of the Lord fell on the people. Hundreds spontaneously fell to the ground. There was concern that they were dead. But after a few hours these same people would come up shouting with great assurance of salvation—then others fell. Between that Sunday and the following Wednesday there were never fewer than five hundred at any given time who lay prostrate on the ground by the power of God.

Both Edwards's sermon and that of the Methodist lay preacher pointed to the reality of God's justice—and how it will be experienced in the future. It is my opinion that God brought the last day (judgment day) forward on these two occasions—for a moment—as a hint of what the final judgment will be like.

To put it another way, these two aforementioned awakenings point to what the effect of the Midnight Cry will be like. As we will see in more detail later in this book, the fear of God will come upon all who hear the message. As fear came upon every soul on the Day of Pentecost (Acts 2:43), so will the fear of the Lord fall on millions all over the world.

God's ultimate wake-up call to His people will be applied accordingly to the wise and the foolish. You must remember that *both* the wise and foolish virgins are asleep in this parable. The wise will be awakened from their slumber. They will be ashamed that they have been caught spiritually asleep and not ready for the Midnight Cry. God will address them by His Word—it will cut right to their hearts—and in an extraordinary manner. This happened initially on the Day of Pentecost (Acts 2:37). The wise virgins will be granted repentance for their being asleep. They will be amazed and extremely grateful that they can be changed to a higher level of glory.

The foolish will be awakened by the same Cry—but only to make them realize they not only were asleep but also have been found out for their failure to pursue God's inheritance for them. Worst of all, like those described in Hebrews 6:4–6, as we will see shortly, they are not granted repentance. Yes, they will be overwhelmed with sorrow—like

Esau who could find no place for repentance though he sought it carefully with tears (Heb. 12:17). Aware of their horrible folly, the foolish will beg the wise for help: "Give us some of your oil, for our lamps have gone out" (Matt. 25:8). But the wise will not be able to help them: "No, lest there not be enough for both us and you. Go rather to those who sell it, and buy some for yourselves" (v. 9).

It will be a terrible moment for those Christians who were not pursuing their inheritance. But for those who faithfully pursue both the Word and the Spirit, the coming of Isaac will bring indescribable joy.

Signs of the Times:
Indications We Are in the Very Last Days

- False teachers masquerading as genuine—Matthew 24:5
- Wars and rumors of wars—Matthew 24:6
- Extreme weather, famines, earthquakes—Matthew 24:7
- Tsunamis—Luke 21:25*
- Increase of wickedness—Matthew 24:12
- Love of most will grow cold—Matthew 24:12
- Gospel preached throughout the world—Matthew 24:14
- God's elect almost deceived by false prophets—Matt.24:24
- Prosperity: buying, selling, planting, building—Luke 17:28
- Heterosexual and homosexual promiscuity—Luke 17:26–29
- Strange diseases—Luke 21:11
- A form of godliness with a denial of its power—2 Timothy 3:5
- An intolerance of sound doctrine—2 Timothy 4:3
- Popularity of teachers who compromise truth—2 Timothy 4:3–4
- Increase of travel—Daniel 12:4
- Increase of knowledge—Daniel 12:4; 2 Timothy 3:7

* Quite apart from tsunamis implied in Jesus's words, "nations will be in anguish and perplexity at the roaring and tossing of the sea" (Luke 21:25, NIV), in the London newspaper *Metro*, dated March 17, 2016, there appeared the headlines: "Biggest Atlantic waves in 65 years." Wave heights were up to "forty percent higher than normal," causing dramatic coastal erosion in Britain, such being the consequence of climate change.

CHAPTER 4

THE IMPORTANCE OF EXPECTANCY

Blessed is that servant whom his master will
find so doing when he comes.
—MATTHEW 24:46

What I say to you I say to all: Watch!
[ESV: "Stay awake!"]
—MARK 13:37

CAN YOU HONESTLY SAY THAT YOU ARE LOOKING FOR THE
coming of the Lord Jesus Christ at the moment? I don't mean
to be unfair, nor do I want to impose a guilt trip on you. Most of us
are understandably very busy and going about our daily duties respon-
sibly and are simply not thinking of the second coming of Jesus. I'm not
saying you should be thinking of the second coming twenty-four hours
a day. But I am trying to be lovingly provocative; I have a mandate to
caution you that we are in very precarious times. And most don't care
a bit.

Have you noticed how few hymns are written nowadays that pertain to the second coming? How many sermons pertain to the need to
be expectant for the second coming? How many sermons point to the
coming judgment? When is the last time you heard a sermon on the
subject of hell and eternal punishment—or even heard them mentioned
in a sermon?

The parable of the ten virgins is an eschatological parable; it refers
to the time of the end before the second coming of Jesus. This is also
known as the Day of the Lord. We have observed also that our parable is
set in Matthew's Gospel between Jesus's teaching of His second coming

in chapter 24 and two other parables that refer to the final judgment in chapter 25.

To restate the premise of my book: the parable of the ten virgins is about the Midnight Cry prior to the second coming. The Midnight Cry is in two phases: (1) the wake-up call and (2) the Spirit of God coming in great power, also known as the spiritual coming of Jesus. The second coming will be in two phases: (1) the spiritual coming of Jesus, when He sends the Spirit of God in great power and makes all His enemies His footstool, and (2) the physical coming of the person of Jesus to the earth when He sets up the final judgment. As I said in the introduction, phase two of the Midnight Cry and phase one of the second coming are the same event.

The purpose of this chapter is to show the utter importance of being ready for the coming Day of the Lord.

ARE YOU NEAR THE DOOR?

One of our more lively and eccentric members at Westminster Chapel was a Nigerian lady named Mary. That is the name she gave herself after being converted from Islam. She had endured torturous persecution back in Nigeria, and to prove it, she has a shriveled hand from being forced to hold it in fire. She has an amazing devotion to Jesus Christ. Noting Jesus's word about being ready for service in Luke 12:35–36, Mary used to say often, "I want to stay near the door."

It is possible to be at the opposite end of the house and not hear the knock at the door when someone you were waiting for comes to see you. "I want to be near the door so I can open it as soon as Jesus knocks on it," she would say. What a pity if a very important person comes to your house and you miss the visitation because you are too far from the door to hear the knock.

You will recall that the parable of the ten virgins immediately follows Jesus's warning about not being ready (Matt. 24:42–51). Some might ask: Why be ready for an event that has been postponed for more than two thousand years? I reply: every generation is responsible for being ready for the Lord to show up—whether it be being ready for answered prayer, the Midnight Cry, or the second coming. In fact, Jesus's command to be ready for service "and keep your lamps burning" (Luke 12:36, NIV) is not referring specifically to an eschatological event. As we will see further below, a reference to the Son of man "coming at an hour you do not expect" need not always refer to the second coming (v. 40). In other words, God wants His people to be expectant for Him to show up in any generation at any time.

A SOBERING PRECEDENT

One of the early examples of not being ready for God's visitation was when the twelve spies returned from Canaan with their report of the Promised Land. There was a unanimous consensus that the land indeed flowed with milk and honey, but ten of the twelve spies, being intimidated, could only lament that the people who lived in Canaan were "strong." Therefore, when Caleb said, "Let us go up at once and possess it, for we are able to overcome it" (Num. 13:30), he was outvoted. The men who had spied with Caleb gave the children of Israel a bad report, saying the people were "men of great stature...and in our eyes we were like grasshoppers, and so we were in their eyes" (vv. 32–33). The majority ruled: the Israelites would not be going into Canaan.

God was very angry with these people. After all, even though those same people had witnessed the historic Passover in Egypt, the extraordinary crossing of the Red Sea on dry land, and other miraculous signs, they refused to listen to Caleb. This was the occasion when God swore an oath, namely, that this generation of people over the age of twenty would not be allowed to enter Canaan. The land of Canaan became a symbol for God's "rest." God swore in His wrath that these people would absolutely and irrevocably not be able to enter His rest (Heb. 3:11). And they never did.

INTRODUCING GOD'S OATH

Yogi Berra is often quoted as saying, "It ain't over till it's over." However, when God swears an oath, it is *over*. That means God will not change His mind—ever. So whether He swears an oath in mercy or does so in His anger, His oath will never be revoked. And when the people of Israel later perceived how angry God was and how foolish they had been, they changed their minds. They thought God would have pity on them and enable them to conquer Canaan. So the next day they said, "We will go up to the place which the LORD has promised, for we have sinned" (Num. 14:40). They did not realize that once God swears an oath, there is nothing—ever—that will cause Him to change His mind.

We may change *our* minds, but God will not change His once He swears an oath.

There are basically two levels of divine communication toward His people: the promise and the oath. Both are equally and absolutely true. According to Hebrews 6:18, there are two immutable things in which it is impossible for God to lie—namely, the promise and the oath. But there are differences between them.

First, a promise is often conditional—either with an *if* or an implied *if.* God promises to do certain things but based upon certain conditions; our obedience, for example. Take this great promise: "If my people, who are called by My name, will humble themselves and pray, and seek My face and turn from their wicked ways, then I will hear from heaven, and will forgive their sin and will heal their land" (2 Chron. 7:14). Second Chronicles 7:14 is one of the most famous promises in the Bible, but it is a *conditional* promise.

The oath, however—once it is uttered—is without further conditions and is irrevocable. In other words, once God swears an *oath*, there is nothing you and I can do to change His mind; no obedience, confession on our part, or pleading with Him will move Him.

That is what the ancient Israelites learned—too late. The result was that the entire population of Israelites over the age of twenty died in the wilderness.

On the other hand, the good news is: if God swears in His *mercy,* likewise nothing will change His mind. The first example of God swearing an oath in mercy was to Abraham: "By Myself I have sworn, says the LORD, because you have done this thing, and have not withheld your son, your only son, I will indeed bless you and I will multiply your descendants as the stars of the heavens and as the sand that is on the seashore" (Gen. 22:16–17). This guaranteed irrevocably and forever that the promise through Isaac would mean not only that Isaac's seed would be as the sand of the sea but also that the seed would culminate in the coming of Jesus Christ (Gal. 3:16).

THE PROMISE AND THE OATH: DIFFERENT YET EQUALLY TRUE

Although both are true, the oath is stronger than the promise. The oath to us means we are guaranteed what is promised *without having to meet any more conditions.* The oath to Abraham concerning Isaac meant it is *over*—that is, no more fretting, worrying, struggling, or working to meet conditions. The oath means that God steps in and says, "Leave it with Me." Abraham could rest in peace that the promise concerning his seed was guaranteed. Done. It's over.

The Israelites had their chance. They blew it. When the opportunity was presented for them to enter into Canaan when they had been in the desert only about two years, they fell into unbelief. There was no excuse for their unbelief. Caleb was so right: "If the LORD delights in us, then He will bring us into this land and give it to us, a land which flows with milk and honey" (Num. 14:8). Why ever could not the rest of the Israelites have seen this? After all, *all* of them witnessed God's mighty power and faithfulness.

When the opportunity came for them to enter Canaan, then, they were not ready. Somehow unbelief settled in. They missed their moment of visitation. They were "far from the door," as my friend Mary would say. All that God had done for them was apparently forgotten. There was an utter absence of expectancy. That is when God swore in His wrath that they would not enter His rest (Heb. 3:11).

This is why expectancy is important. Expectancy is the fruit of an abiding faith. It is also called "hope." There remains faith, hope, and love (1 Cor. 13:13). Hope is faith elevated to confident expectation. We prove our underlying faith by being on tiptoes of expectancy and watchfulness. This is why Jesus urged us to be expectant—not only with reference to His second coming (called the "blessed hope"—Titus 2:13) but regarding *anything* that connects to the possibility of Him showing up.

BEING READY FOR ANSWERED PRAYER

This even means being ready for answered prayer. The point of the parable of the persistent widow is that we must not give up when we pray. This most encouraging parable is introduced with the words: "to illustrate that it is necessary always to pray and not lose heart" (Luke 18:1). The rest of the parable reads by itself, in some ways needing no further comment:

> In a city there was a judge who did not fear God or regard man. And a widow was in that city. She came to him, saying, "Avenge me against my adversary."
>
> He would not for a while. Yet afterward he said to himself, "Though I do not fear God or respect man, yet because this widow troubles me, I will avenge her, lest by her continual coming she will weary me."
>
> And the Lord [Jesus] said, "Hear what the unjust judge says. And shall not God avenge His own elect and be patient with them, who cry day and night to Him? I tell you, He will avenge them speedily. Nevertheless, when the Son of Man comes, will He find faith on the earth?"
>
> —LUKE 18:2–8

Why did Jesus add the bit about the Son of man coming and possibly finding no faith? It is surely an implicit reference to the second coming, but why is this question inserted right *here*? Answer: It is because we often start praying and then give up. We lose expectancy. The reference to the coming of the Son of man refers (1) to the second coming, (2) to any visitation from God, and, most certainly, to (3) answered prayer—when God steps in suddenly to answer the prayer that we asked but may have given up on.

The parable of the widow and the judge is an apt demonstration of the experience of Zechariah, the priest in the temple, who gave up believing that God would answer his prayer. One day, quite unexpectedly, the angel Gabriel showed up with the words: "Your prayer has been heard" (Luke 1:13). Zechariah seemed to have no idea what prayer the angel

Gabriel had in mind! But then Gabriel tells him, "Your wife Elizabeth will bear you a son."

Sadly Zechariah didn't believe a word of it. Gabriel then has to add something that gave no one any pleasure: "And now you will be silent [KJV: "dumb"] and unable to speak until the day that these things happen, because you did not believe my words, which will be fulfilled in their season" (v. 20).

Zechariah had once prayed for a son, but when the son did not come along, after a while Zechariah gave up praying. He gave up praying because he did not believe God heard him. In a word: there was no more expectancy that God would answer him.

Behind Zechariah's experience lies two principles: (1) any prayer that is prayed in the will of God will be answered since asking anything according to "His will" is to be heard (1 John 5:14), and (2) the shape the answered prayer takes is determined by our readiness, or expectancy, when the time comes for that prayer to be answered.

Zechariah was not ready. Even Gabriel's word did not give him any expectancy! But his prayer was answered. And sadly the answered prayer was accompanied with pain and embarrassment. He was struck dumb: unable to speak. His prayer was answered, but he was not allowed to have the full enjoyment of his answer to prayer.

The point of this chapter is to show that expectancy is essential. It is not merely important; it is essential. It is the way God wants us all to live—with expectancy every day of our lives.

Listen to the psalmist: "I wait for the LORD, with bated breath I wait; I long for His Word! My soul waits for the LORD, more than watchmen for the morning, more than watchmen for the morning" (Ps. 130:5–6). The picture here is that of a man stationed on a tower to keep guard over a city during the night. He waits for morning—for that first glimmer of dawn on the horizon. Or consider these words: "As the eyes of servants look to the hand of their master, and as the eyes of a maiden to the hand of her mistress, so our eyes look upon the LORD our God, until He has mercy upon us" (Ps. 123:2). A servant watched the *hand* of his master. He did not look at the master's face. Only the hand. The slightest signal from the master—from snapping a finger or to the subtle turn of the hand—indicated to the servant what to do next. He therefore looked to the master's hand, *expecting* his master to give instructions at any moment. As the servant lived in perpetual watchfulness, so are you and I to live this way all the time.

Therefore, apart from being ready for the second coming or Midnight Cry, the assumption of being ready for God to come *any time*—to show up, turn up, reveal Himself, step in, or take over—lay behind Jesus's teaching.

In other words, Jesus's caution about being watchful, or ready, is nothing new.

ARE YOU READY FOR GOD?

It is one of God's ways—like it or not—to show up or answer prayer when we least expect Him. "Watch therefore, for you do not know what hour your Lord will come" (Matt. 24:42). "The day of the Lord will come like a thief" (2 Pet. 3:10). "For you know perfectly that the day of the Lord will come like a thief in the night" (1 Thess. 5:2). "Look, I am coming as a thief. Blessed is he who watches and keeps his garments on, lest he walk naked and his shame be exposed" (Rev. 16:15).

I find this teaching scary. It is a no-joke thing.

I equally find this teaching thrilling. God is not mocked (Gal. 6:7).

This aspect of God's ways also demonstrates that He wants to have a lively, current, real, two-way relationship with us. He is with us day and night. He is conscious of us day and night. He wants us to be conscious of Him day and night. This means not merely being available to Him should He beckon for us, but to *expect* Him at any time!

I was preaching at the garden tomb in Jerusalem a few years ago. A Scottish couple approached me after the service and said, "Do you recognize us?" I wasn't sure. "You preached a sermon on being ready for answered prayer in our church in Edinburgh. Your sermon made us go back to praying that we might come to the Holy Land one day. We had given up. Your prayer inspired us to keep asking God to let us come here. And here we are! Fancy meeting you here!"

Don't give up hope

Consider the things you have asked God for. Things you have prayed for, asked Him to do for you. Has it occurred to you that you may have actually prayed in the will of God? If so, *that prayer will be answered. But the shape it takes is determined by your expectancy at the time it will be answered.*

Look carefully at 1 John 5:14: "This is the confidence that we have in Him, that if we ask anything according to His will, He hears us." When John refers to God "hearing" us, it is Hebraic type thinking. Every religious Jew knows the *Shema*—"Hear, O Israel: The LORD is our God. The LORD is one!" (Deut. 6:4). The Hebrew *shemar* means both "to hear" and also "to obey." You may have said to your child, "Did you *hear* me?" Because if we truly "hear" in the Hebraic sense, we also obey. So with God. If He "hears" us, it means He will obey our request. But He is sovereign. He can choose when to hear us. And yet if we ask anything in God's will, He hears us. The problem is, we don't always know what God's will is.

That said, John added: "So *if we know* that He hears whatever we ask"—a huge *if*—"we know that we have whatever we asked of Him" (1 John 5:15, emphasis added). How then can we know that God hears us? The answer is: when He swears an oath to us. There are times when we *know* we are being "heard" by the Most High God. In such a case it is "over"—the prayer will be answered. God can reveal this by the immediate witness of His Spirit—conveying to us infallibly that we have been heard.

However, I suspect that being heard in this manner is not common. Indeed, it is, at least in my own experience, rare. It is when God swears an oath to you and you *know*. But in my candid opinion it does not happen every day. It did not happen to Zechariah. He had no idea that many years before, when he and Elizabeth prayed for a son, that they were "heard." Even though they did not know they were heard, the prayer was answered. And even though Zechariah (sadly) did not believe Gabriel, the prayer was still answered. Because any prayer prayed in the will of God will be answered! That is what John affirms in 1 John 5:14.

God *could*, if He chose, swear an oath to us all the time when we pray.

But we might also "coast" on that knowledge and not be as faithful to Him as we might otherwise. I therefore suspect God sometimes withholds swearing an oath to us because "He likes our company"—to quote an expression my friend J. John likes to use—*and* wants us to live day by day in faithful expectancy. This means that we are to make an effort—daily—to live in expectancy.

In my hometown in Ashland, Kentucky, two couples started a church in the south part of town. Many opposed their starting this church, and some made fun of them. "Did you hear about the group in south Ashland? They had eleven people out last Sunday," I remember it being said. But those people prayed that one day they would grow and have their own building. Years later their prayer was answered. One of the loveliest buildings in that part of town was erected, seating four hundred people. They brought in the general superintendent of the denomination to preach the dedicatory sermon. But the very same man whose vision it was to start this church had in the meantime fallen into sin, bitterness, and disgrace. He was not even welcome at this important service. People said that he just drove by the church, seeing all the crowds, but kept going. His prayer was answered, but the shape it took was determined by his expectancy at the time it was answered.

We should note again that the parable of the ten virgins is couched in Jesus's words with regard to being ready (Matt. 24:42–51). There follows Matthew 25:1, NIV, "At that time." Some versions say "Then" (i.e., MEV, ESV, KJV). In other words, in the context of Jesus's warning to be expectant comes this major eschatological parable.

In a word: We are commanded to be ready. To be expectant lest the day this happens takes us by complete surprise. Never forget: one of God's ways is that He frequently shows up when we least expect Him. "I come like a thief!" (Rev. 16:15, NIV).

This is why Jesus admonished us: "Stay awake" (Mark 13:35, ESV). It is God's prerogative to come when we least expect Him.

THE MIDNIGHT CRY IS GOD SWEARING AN OATH

Why is this teaching relevant to the parable of the ten virgins? It is because God *swore an oath* in the Midnight Cry! It was too late for the foolish virgins to get more oil—to pursue the Spirit. It was too late for the foolish to become wise. When this takes place, you will witness countless people who will bitterly regret their spiritual laziness. They will experience the horrible reality that it is too late for them to enjoy the move of the Spirit.

If you ask, Why is God like that?, I answer: It is because He is a jealous God (Exod. 34:14). He wants our undivided attention. All the time. That is simply the way He is.

We cannot say we have not been warned.

CHAPTER 5

A MIXED CHURCH

Five of [the virgins] were wise and five were foolish. Those
who were foolish took their lamps, but took no oil with
them. But the wise took jars of oil with their lamps.
—MATTHEW 25:2–4

I could not speak to you as to spiritual men, but as to worldly,
even as to babes in Christ...for you are still worldly. Since there
is envy, strife, and divisions among you, are you not worldly
and behaving as mere men?...It is actually reported that there
is sexual immorality among you, and such immorality as is not
even named among the Gentiles, that a man has his father's
wife....Deliver him to Satan for the destruction of the flesh, so
that the spirit may be saved on the day of the Lord Jesus.
—1 CORINTHIANS 3:1, 3; 5:1, 5

YOU WILL RECALL THAT IN THE ANCIENT MIDDLE EASTERN
weddings there would be young unmarried ladies who served as
bridesmaids. Young unmarried ladies in those days would be virgins. In
any case, Jesus refers to them as virgins. The ten virgins typify the bride.
They are called virgins because of their purity. Because the righteousness of Christ is imputed to those who become a part of Christ's bride,
the church is seen by God as pure. In a word: the ten virgins typify the
regenerate people of God.

But not all who become a part of the bride of Christ turn out the
same way. As we have seen, all Christians are called to enter into their
inheritance. Some do; some don't. Sadly only some are wise; some are
foolish. Inheritance is one of the New Testament terms for what you get
from God as a reward for obedience. This does not mean that you "earn"
something from God, but that you are worthy of what God wants to

give you. Those in the parable who pursue their inheritance are called wise virgins. Those who don't are called foolish virgins.

Can a true Christian be foolish? Yes.

You cannot lose your salvation, but you can lose your inheritance. God will never take away the righteousness that He has imputed to you, but He will deny you the reward that is promised to you had you been obedient. God will never abort the life that has been imparted to you—after all, it is His life. The eternal life of God in your soul is what enables you to know God in an intimate manner. But not all come to know Him in an intimate manner. To those foolish virgins who do not take oil in their lamps there will come a sad moment: the Lord will deny knowing you when you come begging for a part in the great celebration.

Not all Christians will have a part in the wedding banquet referred to in Matthew 25:10. Only those who pursued knowing the Lord intimately, namely, the wise virgins who took oil in their lamps, will have a part in this great celebration.

As there are two kinds of faith, so also are there two levels of knowing God. The first level of knowing Him is bestowed on all who have been born again. The new birth is an introduction to God's ways. We are "in Christ" (2 Cor. 5:17). We do not "lack any spiritual gift" (1 Cor. 1:7, NIV). After all, we have the Holy Spirit. Once the life of God is imparted to us, we have a taste of the true knowledge of God. This means we have in us the potential for all the gifts and fruit of the Spirit.

We likewise have assurance of salvation. We will all go to heaven one day. Therefore because we have been regenerated, we are privileged to know the God of the Bible—that He is holy, just, gracious, sovereign, omnipotent, omniscient, and omnipresent. Therefore *all who are saved know the Lord*; that is, to some degree. All of us have faith in measure (Rom. 12:3).

But not all who are saved pursue Him with diligence so that they get to know Him *intimately*. Knowing the Lord intimately comes by walking in the light (1 John 1:7). It comes by resisting temptation (James 1:12). It comes from not grieving the Holy Spirit (Eph. 4:30). Those who earnestly pursue their inheritance will get to know God's ways by an intimate experience of Him. In other words: they are the wise virgins who take oil in their lamps. Those who don't take oil in their lamps not only forfeit knowing God intimately but also will hear Him say to them, "I do not know you" (Matt. 25:12). Of course He knew them in one sense—just as the gatekeeper of the ancient Middle Eastern wedding knew all the invited guests. But the horrible word to those who blew away their inheritance will be: "I do not know you"; that is, at the deeper level of intimacy to which all Christians are called.

There has been a long controversy in church history as to *what* the church is and *who* makes up the church. The church is often described as (1) where the Word of God is preached and (2) where the sacraments are administered. Some would add to this: (3) where discipline is exercised; that is, excommunicating those who are not faithful.

The distinction is sometimes made between the visible church and the invisible church. The visible church would be all those who have professed faith in Christ whether or not they are regenerate (born again). The invisible church would be only the regenerate—God's elect—whom God alone knows.

As for the parable of the ten virgins, some interpreters would say that the "wise" virgins alone are saved; the "foolish" are not saved. They would say that the wise virgins are the invisible church; the wise *and* foolish comprise the visible church. I don't agree with this interpretation.

Keep in mind that the lamp refers to the Word; the oil refers to the Spirit.

Remember that all the virgins—foolish and wise—represent saved people: (1) Virginity denotes purity, suggesting that righteousness has been imputed to all and that both wise and foolish virgins are regarded by God as pure. (2) The foolish virgins obviously had oil in their lamps since they later say that their "lamps have gone out" (Matt. 25:8). Oil means they had the Holy Spirit, and only the Holy Spirit can give life (John 6:63). Anyone who does not have the Spirit of Christ does not belong to Him (Rom. 8:9), but these *did* have the Holy Spirit. The foolish virgins in the parable therefore symbolize those who had been converted. Their malady was not never *having* the Sprit but not *pursuing* the Spirit: they did not take more oil with them as the wise virgins had done.

To bring in the concept of the visible church (wise and foolish) and the invisible church (wise only) does not fit the parable of the ten virgins. That said, it is certainly possible—and it happens all the time—for a person to join the church and not be regenerate. A person can make a profession of faith and not be saved. A person can walk down an aisle at the end of a sermon and not be born again. He can kneel at an altar and weep and not know the gospel. A person can be baptized and not have saving faith. People can take Holy Communion without having been converted. People can join a church and stay in a church for all manner of reasons.

IMPORTANT CLARIFICATION

Not all who go to church are Christians. Not all who make a profession of faith are truly born again. And yet, in our parable, both the wise and foolish do represent the *invisible* church. The phrase *invisible church* refers to the way God sees His people—which may not be visible to us. The invisible church refers to God's elect. The Lord alone knows those who are His (2 Tim. 2:19). For even the foolish virgins are part of God's elect. They will go to heaven. But not all the elect pursue their inheritance as they should. And because some of them foolishly blow away their inheritance, they will lose a reward at the judgment seat of Christ. They suffer loss of reward, but, as we saw above, they will be saved (1 Cor. 3:14–15).

So in the parable of the ten virgins all the virgins are to be seen as saved, but not all pursue the Holy Spirit. Their folly will be exposed when the Midnight Cry comes.

Some may ask: What about those who fell away in Hebrews 6:4–6? It reads:

> For it is impossible for those who were once enlightened, who have tasted the heavenly gift, who shared in the Holy Spirit, and have tasted the good word of God and the powers of the age to come, if they fall away, to be renewed once more to repentance, since they again crucify to themselves the Son of God and subject Him to public shame.

The people in Hebrews 6:4–6 are true Christians. First, the four descriptions (enlightened, tasted of Christ, tasted the word of God, and tasted the powers of the coming age) show they not only have been converted but also have made considerable progress.

If you say they only "tasted" (but did not digest), I answer: Christ "tasted" death for every man (Heb. 2:9, NIV); does this mean He did not really die? Of course He did. Those who "tasted" were truly converted.

Second, they had previously repented. Notice the words: they could not be "brought back to repentance" (Heb. 6:6, NIV). This means they had repented once. They could not be renewed "once more" (Gr. *palin*). They may have repented many times in the past. But at some point they crossed over a line—and God swore in His wrath—and could therefore never come back to the grace of repentance.

Do not think that the "foolish" virgins are necessarily those who may be half-hearted Christians and live close to the world. No doubt people like this are certainly foolish virgins. But it is equally possible that some of those who appear the most faithful, the godliest, and the most committed are still foolish virgins. How is it possible? I answer: They are like those in the church of Laodicea—lukewarm. Smug. They know it all. Have need of nothing. But they have no objectivity about themselves. Said Jesus: "Yet [you] do not realize that you are wretched, miserable, poor, blind, and naked" (Rev. 3:17). To put it another way, some of those who seem so "pious" and high profile in the church are enemies of the current move of the Holy Spirit.

You will ask: If they are saved, what happens to them when they fall away? I reply: They become stone deaf to the Holy Spirit. The context of this passage begins in Hebrews 5:11 when the writer warns that they have already become "hard of hearing." This means they were already hard of hearing but, so far, short of becoming stone deaf to the Spirit. They could hear, yes; but only just. However, this dullness of hearing could lead to the utter inability to hear at all—the worst scenario. They remain saved, yes, but they no longer hear God speak. This is why the writer warned earlier, "Today, if you hear His voice, do not harden your hearts" (Heb. 3:7–8).

I will say that as a pastor of some years I believe I have known people like this. I am not their judge of course. But in my heart of hearts I believe I have known people just like those described in Hebrews 6:4–6. That said, they will be in heaven. It would be wrong to say either (1) they were never saved or (2) they could lose their salvation. There are many people like this in the church: truly born again but who foolishly forfeited their inheritance.

The worst scenario for a true Christian is to become totally deaf to the Holy Spirit. Such a person forfeits being changed from glory to glory as described in 2 Corinthians 3:18. I say all this in more detail in my book *Are You Stone Deaf to the Spirit or Rediscovering God?* (an exposition of Hebrews 6). In a word: they do not lose their salvation but they lose their inheritance.

In the case of the foolish virgins they realized their folly of not pursuing the Spirit. But they realized it too late.

With this being said, the characteristics of both foolish and wise virgins are listed below.

Ten Characteristics of a Foolish Virgin

- One who has little or no concern for daily prayer and Bible reading
- One who walks in bitterness and unforgiveness and feels no conviction of sin for this
- One who is not accountable to fellow believers
- One who does not walk in all the light God gives him or her
- One who does not put himself under Holy Scripture but considers himself the exception and puts himself above the Word
- One who does not welcome the counsel and caring rebukes of godly people
- One who pursues the fruit of the Spirit but not the gifts, as with some Word people
- One who emphasizes the gifts of the Spirit but does not pursue the fruit, as with some Spirit people
- One who is happy merely to be saved but who does not care about a reward at the judgment seat of Christ
- One who does not develop a true sensitivity to the ways of the Holy Spirit

In a word: foolish virgins are those who do not care sufficiently to come into their inheritance. They will be saved by fire at the judgment seat of Christ and lose their reward (1 Cor. 3:14–15).

Ten Characteristics of a Wise Virgin

- One who has a disciplined life of daily prayer and Bible reading
- One who walks in total forgiveness
- One who is accountable to fellow believers
- One who walks in all the light God gives him or her
- One who submits totally to Holy Scripture
- One who welcomes the counsel and rebukes of godly people
- One who pursues the fruit of the Spirit but also the gifts
- One who pursues not only the gifts of the Spirit but also the fruit
- One who cares deeply about a reward at the judgment seat of Christ
- One who develops a genuine sensitivity to the ways of the Holy Spirit

In a word: wise virgins are those who are determined to come into their inheritance and thus receive a reward at the judgment seat of Christ.

CHAPTER 6

THE DELAY

The bridegroom was a long time in coming [MEV, ESV: "delayed"].
—MATTHEW 25:5, NIV

But if that evil servant says in his heart, "My master delays his
coming," and begins to strike his fellow servants and eat and drink
with the drunkards, the master of that servant will come on a day
when he does not look for him and in an hour he is not aware of
and will cut him in pieces and appoint him his portion with the
hypocrites, where there shall be weeping and gnashing of teeth.
—MATTHEW 24:48–51

THE DELAY OF THE COMING OF THE BRIDEGROOM HAS LASTED OVER
two thousand years so far. No one in the first century remotely
conceived that Jesus would remain at the right hand of God for more
than two thousand years. They thought His return would be in their
lifetime. The two angels on Mount Olivet assured the disciples that
Jesus would return in the same way as they saw Him go into heaven
(Acts 1:10–11). I suspect they thought He would be back in a week or
two. Or a few months at the most. Well, at least in the same generation. Indeed, as we will see further below, so expectant were Christians
in Thessalonica that Paul had to write a second letter to them to say
"that Day will not come" until certain things took place first: (1) the
rebellion, or falling away; and (2) the man of lawlessness, or man of sin,
is revealed (2 Thess. 2:3). Countless words have been written over the
centuries—especially in the twentieth century—as to the meaning of
the "falling away" and the "man of sin." Not a few writers have given
their opinion on the latter—ranging from Hitler to Stalin, from the
pope to Barack Obama!

It is surely good—and healthy—when Christians expect to see the second coming of Jesus in their own day. That shows they are expectant. I have known several people to whom it was "revealed" that they would be alive at the time of the second coming. All those are now with the Lord. It is so easy to think something is revealed to you by the Lord when it is precisely what you want so much! I too have grown up assuming I myself will be alive when Jesus comes back again. I have not given up hope either, but I know it may not happen during my lifetime. However, I do hope at least to see the initial fallout from the Midnight Cry.

Why the delay? After all, this could not be by accident. It is not that things have gone wrong—or that God is waiting on us to do something to make His coming take place. First, the very parable of the ten virgins hints of a delay. It is part of the plan. The Lord never said He would be coming back in a few days. Jesus chose the parable of the ten virgins and did not overlook the fact that sometimes the bridegroom in the ancient Middle Eastern weddings would be awhile in coming. This was assumed. The bridesmaids had no idea how long they would have to wait; they were only told to be ready. Jesus therefore referred to this possibility and did so because the Father directed Him specifically to say it. Jesus said only what the Father told Him to say (John 5:19). Whereas Jesus Himself did not know the day or the hour, He made it clear that *the Father knows* (Matt. 24:36).

Never forget this: our heavenly Father knows the exact day and time of day the second coming will take place. It was the Father therefore who spoke through Jesus that the day will be a "long time in coming." It was for our good and benefit lest we become demoralized or disillusioned that it has taken so long.

It is very important that we realize that God *the Father* knows the day and the hour of Jesus's coming. Why? This is because it is essential that we know there is a *date on the calendar*—still future—when Jesus will come. I recognize that some good and sincere people believe that we can hasten the day by our prayers and evangelistic efforts. In a sense they are right. For we need to realize that one of the signs of the times is that the gospel will reach all nations before the end. Therefore the sooner we can get the gospel to all peoples of the earth, the sooner Jesus will come. So in that sense, yes, we can speed His coming.

That said, it is still a fixed date in the future. Only God the Father knows. Jesus for some reason added that not even the angels know the day (Matt. 24:36). Why did He mention angels? You tell me. So—in a word: neither Jesus nor the angels but *only the Father* knows the day. This fact was somewhat repeated when Jesus disappointed His disciples with His answer to them just before He ascended to heaven. They wanted to know if He was going to restore the kingdom to Israel at that time. The idea of Messiah restoring the kingdom to Israel was part of their almost inflexible mind-set. So they wanted to know if Jesus was going to do this—*then*. Jesus deftly avoided addressing their obsession but said, "It is not for you to know times or the dates, which the Father has fixed by His own authority" (Acts 1:7). Whatever else this means, it shows that there are times "fixed" by the Father.

Why is this important? It is partly because the teaching of the omniscience of God is at stake. God either knows everything—past, present, future—or He doesn't. This absolutely means He knows the future as well as He knows the past—or He doesn't. But He *does* know everything. He *does* know the future as perfectly as He knows the past. Our heavenly Father does not learn anything—ever. He already knows *everything*.

I ask again: Why is this so important? It is because this addresses a deadly heresy that has crept into some circles—called open theism. Once you capitulate to open theism, you abandon the very foundation of prophecy. Open theism purports that God does not know the future—only the present. He even looks to us for input to know what to do next! This teaching is man-centered and denies the absolute sovereignty of God. Prophecy is based upon the premise that God absolutely, totally, and infallibly knows the future. If God did not know the time Jesus would be born, then a vast portion of the Old Testament would be irrelevant. Jesus was born in the "fullness of time" (Gal. 4:4). The Father knew the date of Jesus's first coming all along. So too with the second coming, the Father knows the day and the hour it will happen.

He also knows the time of the Midnight Cry, which will happen sometime prior to the second coming. What is more, the Father knew this when He led His Son to give us the parable of the ten virgins. Thus the phrase that the bridegroom's coming was "delayed"—a long time coming—was stated so that we all would know that the last two thousand years has not taken God by surprise. The parable that follows—the parable of the talents—includes the same point—a delay. It is somewhat parallel with the parable of the ten virgins. It is about a man going on a journey and "after a long time" he returned (Matt. 25:19, NIV).

But why the delay? Only God knows for sure. I'm glad that the second coming did not take place before 1935 or I would not have been born! I could add that I am glad it did not take place before April 5, 1942—the day I was converted at the age of six. So with you. God knew you from the foundation of the world. He loves every person, said St. Augustine, as though there were no one else to love. God has a family so vast that "no one could count" them (Rev. 7:9). But God knows every one of them. Some of them were born in 5000 BC. Some 500 BC. Some AD 100. And some AD 2000. In a word: part of the delay in Jesus's second coming has been to allow time for all His people to be born and be saved.

God has His own reasons why He has not instructed His Son to leave His throne before now. Peter prophesied that men would scoff at this kind of teaching. "There shall come scoffers in the last days who walk after their own lusts, and say, 'Where is the promise of His coming? For since the fathers fell asleep, all things have continued as they were since the beginning of the creation'" (2 Pet. 3:3–4). Be careful, dear reader, that you don't join the rank of scoffers.

The Father therefore knew at the time when Jesus gave the parable of the ten virgins there would be a *long* delay. And so it has been.

But this delay will end. When? "No one knows," said Jesus (Matt. 24:36).

I am acutely aware that previous generations of godly people were convinced Jesus would come in their day. I noted earlier that Jonathan Edwards even believed that the revival in New England in his day was part of the outpouring of the Spirit before the end. There have always been those who thought Jesus would come in their day—and that surely He would not wait this long.

But He has. Am I therefore going to give up believing Jesus is coming soon—and the Midnight Cry is at hand? No. And don't you. Jesus is coming again. It is still future. He has not come yet. And the greatest move of the Holy Spirit since Pentecost is coming any day now.

CHAPTER 7

THE SLEEPING CHURCH

*The bridegroom was a long time in coming, and
they all became drowsy and fell asleep.*
—MATTHEW 25:5, NIV

*So then, let us not be like others, who are
asleep, but let us be awake and sober.*
—1 THESSALONIANS 5:6, NIV

THERE ARE MANY WAYS TO DESCRIBE TODAY'S CHURCH. DR. A. W. Tozer said, "If the Holy Spirit was withdrawn from the church today, 95 percent of what we do would go on and no one would know the difference. If the Holy Spirit had been withdrawn from the New Testament church, 95 percent of what they did would stop, and everybody would know the difference."[1] Dr. Martyn Lloyd-Jones often said that today's church is best described with one word: *superficiality*. He used to say to me, "We are living in the period of the Book of Judges; everyone does what seems right in their own eyes." Dr. J. I. Packer has described American Christianity as "a thousand miles wide and one inch deep."[2] A Chinese pastor was asked for his opinion of American Christianity, having been given a tour of several megachurches in the United States, and he replied, "I am amazed at how much the church in America can accomplish without the Holy Spirit."[3]

Jesus's own description of the church in the very last days is summed up in one word: *asleep*. This of course means being spiritually asleep. Synonyms for being asleep are being numb, insensible, unfeeling, or even comatose. Being asleep is the opposite of alertness, liveliness, or being "on the boil." Since the parable of the ten virgins is prophetic, and if indeed we are in the very last days, we should not be surprised that the church of our generation is asleep. That is the most apt description

I can think of to describe the church in general today. There are some happy exceptions. There are bright spots in the world where Christians are vibrant and full of expectancy. There are those churches in which the goal of the leadership and the people is to see both the Word and Spirit function in great measure and in equal proportion. These things said, I would nonetheless express my view that the church today, generally speaking, is spiritually asleep.

Jesus repeatedly warned, "Stay awake" (Mark 13:35, ESV).

I have long been intrigued—I still don't entirely understand it—how Jesus's inner circle (Peter, James, and John) were overcome by sleepiness on two of the most important occasions of the entire ministry of Jesus. First, at the transfiguration. Jesus's clothing became dazzling white. Moses and Elijah appeared. They spoke about Jesus's departure, which He was about to accomplish in Jerusalem. And would you believe it: Peter, James, and John were heavy with *sleep* (Luke 9:32)! Of all times to be asleep!

Second, when Jesus was praying in Gethsemane. At the very time when Jesus needed them the most, the same three men slept through it all! He pleaded with them to watch with Him for one hour. But they kept falling asleep. Jesus gave up hope that they would stay awake and said, "Sleep on now" (Matt. 26:45). I don't quite grasp the meaning of these three men being asleep on such important occasions. And yet, although Peter, James, and John were literally asleep on these extraordinary occasions, I do wonder if it possibly points to the spiritual sleep of the church today when—more than ever—we need to be awake. Never has there been such a need for the church to be alert. But we are asleep.

It needs to be repeated that the parable of the ten virgins shows *both* the wise and the foolish as being asleep. "They all"—wise and foolish—became drowsy and fell sleep (Matt. 25:5).

CHARACTERISTICS OF SLEEP

There are three obvious things about sleep.

1. We do not know we are asleep until we wake up!

This factor concerning sleep can be both funny and scary. The funny thing is, you can lie down to rest with the utter determination not to sleep but with the intent only to let your mind and body rest a moment or two. Then comes the shock—you slept for an hour! But you had no idea you were asleep until you woke up.

In the natural this might be funny, but in the spiritual it is scary. I believe most Christians today have no idea that they are asleep *spiritually*; they won't know this until they get an effectual wake-up call. If I told most of the readers of this book, "You are asleep," you would probably feel insulted and become defensive. But the truth is that no one is aware they are sleeping while they are asleep.

The problem with spiritual sleep is that it can go on and on indefinitely. Physical sleep may last a few hours, but we do wake up eventually. However, spiritual sleep can go on and on indefinitely—even for years—unless we get an effective wake-up call.

Whereas physical sleep meets a need, spiritual sleep is never good. You are out of touch with what should grip you, detached from what God wants to do today, largely unconcerned about the state of the world, and tolerant of things that should give you a sense of outrage. It means you are virtually lifeless. Whereas physical sleep does replenish the body, spiritual sleep does not replenish the soul. In fact, it is soul-destroying. If God did not graciously step in, we never would never wake up.

Spiritual sleep is not the same as being backslidden. And yet it may appear to be that at times. Backsliding can be by degrees. We all have times like this. I certainly have. But it is unhealthy for anyone not to be watching and ready. The best of Christians get discouraged or become complacent. The wise virgins in the parable are not in a seriously backslidden state but are nonetheless spiritually asleep. These sleeping wise virgins are granted repentance because the *bent of their lives is walking in the light and pursuing their inheritance*. The term *backslider*—referring to one who slips back or falls—applies to a Christian. Backsliders have something to slip back from; they have tasted the goodness of the Lord and have thus been converted. But they have gone "off the boil," as my British friends would say. In other words, they've lost their passion.

The backslider is "filled with his own ways" (Prov. 14:14). The ESV says "filled with the fruit of his ways." When we are filled with our own ways, we cannot be reasoned with. We are usually unapproachable. Again, we are like the Laodiceans, convinced that we "have need of nothing" (Rev. 3:17). We can see backsliding in others; we cannot see it in ourselves. But if we do see it in others, we are told to approach a person gently but while considering ourselves lest we too become like that (Gal. 6:1).

There are degrees of backsliding as also there are levels and depths of sleep. If one is barely asleep, one wakes up easily. But if one is in a very deep slumber, he can sleep through a violent storm; he cannot even hear it thunder.

There are basically two kinds of backsliding. There is overt backsliding—like committing adultery. Overt backsliding brings disgrace upon the name of Christ. As a pastor I have had to deal with Christians being overtaken with the sin of adultery. Sometimes they will admit that they are doing what is wrong; sometimes they seem utterly impervious to what they are doing. The most difficult type of backslider to reach is one overtaken with self-righteousness. Even people living in adultery can be self-righteous; they feel entitled, that God understands their situation and that they are the exception to the general rule.

On the other hand, there is backsliding that is not so recognizable. Take, for example, people who hold a grudge and refuse to forgive. This kind of backsliding may be hidden from others. These people do not bring disgrace on Christ's name like the adulterous, but they can be a hindrance to the work of the Holy Spirit. And yet because they are not living in open, blatant sin, they often refuse to see a problem in themselves. The consequence is, often, that they become self-righteous. Self-righteous people may be outwardly moral and be faithful in church attendance. And yet they can be almost impossible to reach; they absolutely feel good about themselves, not knowing they are smug, detached, and cold. They feel totally entitled to God's blessing. People like this seldom see themselves with objectivity. It takes a wake-up call from God that turns them around.

This has happened to me. More than once! When I have been overtaken with a sin of bitterness, for example, people have had to be very careful with me. I am on the defensive. I think they are impertinent to suggest I could be in the wrong. But if the person approaches me in the right spirit and with a lot of wisdom, I am sometimes mercifully able to see my blindness, recalcitrance, and coldness. When I see this, I wake up and am astonished that I could be in that position! Some readers may recall how I've shared in other books that Josif Tson lovingly but firmly said to me in my darkest hour, "RT, you must *totally forgive them*; unless you *totally forgive them*, you will be in chains." I thank God for this wake-up call.

I have been shocked lately to learn of several churches in America and Great Britain that are known to tolerate all sorts of sexual promiscuity. These are highly respected Evangelical churches where premarital sex, gay sex, and other highly questionable practices are going on—with the full knowledge of the pastoral leadership. Often nothing is said about it, much less is it addressed firmly from the pulpit. One prominent pastor, however, recently preached a strong sermon against premarital sex— which shook up many in his congregation—and then put the sermon on the church's website. But he took it off in one week because so many complained. There are a vast number of churches—I wish it were not true—wherein the gifts of the Spirit are exercised, especially speaking in tongues, but that apparently allow sexual misconduct to carry on lest the people stop coming to church. When I was in Singapore, I found out firsthand of a huge church in which the pastor's wife has carried on sensuous dancing—almost naked—before the congregation. I saw it on YouTube. This was condoned because it "reaches people for the gospel." It is an example of "hyper-grace" teaching, which claims we do not need to confess our sins since Jesus paid for them on the cross!

Are *you* involved in anything like this? Have you condoned this sort of behavior? Are you having an affair at this moment? Are you doing things that the New Testament clearly condemns? Are you? I come to you on bended knee with this word: STOP! Stop it now. Break it off. Do not delay.

God is gracious. He knows how to reach us when we are in a cold and inwardly backslidden state.

However, I doubt that the Midnight Cry will come like a gentle approach to a sleeping church. It could be that way, were God to treat the church according to the principle of Galatians 6:1—when we find a fellow Christian overtaken in a fault, we should restore them gently lest we too be tempted. But I suspect it will not be like that. I expect the Midnight Cry to be more like September 11—a sudden and tremendous shock that wakes us all up out of a deep sleep.

To the wise virgins who are awakened, they will be truly horrified that they would allow this sad state to happen to them. They will be ashamed. Smitten. Repentant. But at the same time they will be so grateful that God has graciously awakened them from their sleep.

The foolish virgins in the parable are exposed not so much for being asleep as for not having pursued both the Word and Spirit. They took no oil in their lamps. We have seen that it was not that there was no oil in their lamps, for they later said, "Our lamps have gone out" (Matt. 25:8). They apparently felt no need for *more* oil until it was too late.

Perhaps the foolish virgins represent Christians whose thinking is similar to the old Brylcreem slogan: "A little dab will do you." Some of you may remember this saying from the old commercials for Brylcreem, a hair product that helps your hair comb better and stay in place. An old friend of mine had a sermon he called "Brylcreem Religion." It was intended to expose superficial Christians who did not want too much spirituality; only a "dab."

I suspect the foolish virgins were like that when it comes to the Spirit. The wise took more oil; the foolish did not. I would not want to press the analogy too far, but it does make one think of those Christians who want the Word—and nothing more. The notion of pursuing the Spirit—as seeking the gifts and fruit of the Spirit—is not their cup of tea. Strange as it may seem, some Christians for some reason seem to be afraid of the Holy Spirit.

2. We do things in our sleep we would not do when awake.

In your dreams you do things that would be unthinkable for you when awake. Sigmund Freud would say that dreams come from unexpressed subconscious desires or fears. Perhaps. I know I have dreams of doing things that I would never do if I were awake. Some are embarrassing. Some are ridiculous. I only know what it is to have awful dreams, sometimes bizarre. It does not matter whether a dream is based upon a wish fulfillment or fear; I will leave that to the psychologists. My point is, the best of the people of God do things in their dreams they would not do when awake. They are often embarrassed by what they dreamed of doing.

So it is with spiritual sleep. When we are not consciously watching for God's visitation, we are vulnerable to backsliding. When we are not awake and ready, we sometimes, however slowly, let innocent but ominous things creep in. Often it is the small things such as work, being defensive when people want to help us, or not reading the Bible or having quiet time with the Lord. It can even be legitimate things such as making more phone calls or spending more time with well-connected people. After a while one rationalizes and little by little accepts opinions, habits, or behavior he thought would never happen to him! And yet the heart is, after all, "more deceitful than all things and desperately wicked" (Jer. 17:9). The godliest person on earth is capable of the most heinous kind of sin if he or she is not on guard.

Always keep in mind that even the wise virgins were asleep in this parable. This means that those pursing the Word and Spirit may be asleep.

"Backsliding begins in the knees," we used to say back in Kentucky. It was a way of saying that your time in prayer and the Word of God is cut short because you are too busy. When a job or schedule change in your life makes it seemingly impossible to pray, you say to yourself, "God understands. I will get back to praying one day. I will start back in church one day. I will support the church one day."

The shocking thing is, when we begin to rationalize our behavior, we pick up bad habits; compromised behavior, ungodly attitudes, and bitterness elbow their way in and the old lifestyle takes over. Television becomes more important than our prayer and devotional life. Entertainment becomes essential to our lifestyle. The months turn into years. After a while this can lead some of us into a major slip and fall— into sexual sin, carnal ambition, loss of honesty, and a lack of integrity. It all starts by telling ourselves, "This is only for a time." Or, "This is a one-off." Or whatever.

The wake-up call will bring us to our senses. We will be utterly distraught that we could have slipped so far, that we degenerated to a worldly lifestyle—even paralleling the way we were before being converted. Yes, that happens.

Am I saying that a person who pursues both the Word and the Spirit could fall asleep and indulge in carnal things? Yes. But hopefully only temporarily. Peter, James, and John became fully awake at Jesus's transfiguration and saw His glory. We have all done this sort of thing if we are totally honest.

After all, backsliding is by degrees. You can imagine it on a scale of 1 to 10, from what seems harmless (1) to what is disgraceful (10). Who has not backslidden to some degree? An example of a level 1 might be getting your feelings hurt, sulking, indifference, or skipping prayer time for a while. A level 10 would be sexual sin—doing things that bring great dishonor to God's name.

Never forget that King David—a man after God's own heart—committed adultery and murder (2 Sam. 11). But he was forgiven (2 Sam. 12). He was also restored (Ps. 51). When Nathan the prophet confronted David, repentance followed. The proof that a person was following the Word and Spirit is that repentance is granted. But when a person was not following the Word and Spirit—being like the foolish virgins—repentance is not granted, as we will see below.

What is perhaps most worrisome about the state of the church nowadays is that we have become so used to the moral decline of society around us that it no longer bothers us as it once did. We just roll over and go back to sleep—whether it be drug trafficking, violence owing to racism, ever-increasing terrorism, young girls being kidnapped and forced into prostitution, or pornography becoming more and more explicit on television. The list goes on and on. Where is the sense of outrage?

One highly respected church in America made available on their website a fairly well-known lady speaking to a vast audience of young people. I'm not sure why she did it, but, when making reference to the angels in heaven who rest not day or night saying "Holy, holy, holy" before the throne of God, she implied that angels must get bored doing this. So they send texts to one another and have "farting contests." The audience laughed their heads off, thinking it was hilarious. There was no outrage.

We are asleep.

3. We hate the sound of an alarm.

This would be especially true of the foolish virgins. In my pastoral experience, when one has to face a rebellious person—especially one living in immorality—or even an upstanding church member whose attitude has become very negative, an effort to wake them up is met with resentment. They don't like the intrusion of a point of view that would require a change in their lifestyle or attitude.

However, I would have thought that the wise virgins would *welcome* the wake-up call. Indeed, the backslidden person whose heart basically pursues the Word and Spirit will be thankful to the person who approaches him or her. He may be defensive at first. But a truly spiritual man or woman *wants to know* if he or she has gotten it wrong and is spiritually asleep. A wake-up call *could* be what we saw above as internal chastening—through the Word. Or it could be external chastening—when God has to get our attention other ways. Therefore I reckon that the person whose bent of life has been the pursuit of the Word and Spirit, though he might be defensive at first, will welcome a wake-up call from the Holy Spirit with both hands.

Signs That the Church Is Spiritually Asleep

- Absence of conviction of sin
- A lack of the fear of God
- No sense of outrage over the godlessness of society
- Watching pornography and feeling justified
- Avarice, greed, and lack of financial integrity
- No outrage over the church's lack of credibility in the world
- No concern about people going to hell
- Little concern about lack of knowledge of God's Word
- Indifference to holding grudges and unforgiveness
- Indifference to talking to people about Christ
- Tolerating heresies like open theism and hyper-grace teaching
- Indifference to the teaching that the Bible is infallible
- Indifference to how much time is spent in prayer and quiet time

It is my prayer that this book might serve as a mini wake-up call in advance of *the* wake-up call down the road—the Midnight Cry. If these lines can be used of the Holy Spirit to get someone back on the rails, one of the main purposes of my writing it is accomplished.

Is it possible that you have been asleep spiritually? Or are asleep now?

CHAPTER 8

COMMON GRACE, ISRAEL, AND A SLEEPING WORLD

You are the salt of the earth. But if the salt loses its saltiness, how shall it be made salty? It is from then on good for nothing but to be thrown out and to be trampled underfoot by men. You are the light of the world. A city that is set on a hill cannot be hidden.
—MATTHEW 5:13–14

Awake, you who sleep, arise from the dead,
and Christ will give you light.
—EPHESIANS 5:14

I WOULD NOT GO TO THE STAKE FOR THE PREMISE THAT GREAT Britain or the United States of America has thrived under a special relationship with God—somewhat like that of Israel. But I cannot deny that some parallels can be drawn between these two nations and Israel. That said, we know that Israel generally, and Jerusalem in particular, has been under a special covenant with God. For example:

For you are a holy people to the LORD your God. The LORD your God has chosen you to be His special people, treasured above all peoples who are on the face of the earth.
—DEUTERONOMY 7:6

I have chosen Jerusalem for My name to dwell there.
—2 CHRONICLES 6:6

For he who touches you [Jerusalem] touches the apple of His eye.
—ZECHARIAH 2:8

For I could wish that I myself were accursed from Christ for my brothers, my kinsmen by race, who are Israelites, to whom belong the adoption, the glory, the covenants, the giving of the law, the service of God, and the promises, to whom belong the patriarchs, and from whom, according to the flesh, is Christ, who is over all, God forever blessed. Amen.

—ROMANS 9:3–5

THE FAMILY OF GOD

Jesus called His disciples the "salt of the earth" (Matt. 5:13). God has had a family since He created Adam and Eve in the Garden of Eden. Paul said, "For this reason I bow my knees to the Father of our Lord Jesus Christ, from whom the whole family in heaven and earth is named" (Eph. 3:14–15). God's family is called by various names: the people of God, those who were a part of God's covenant, the elect or chosen of God. Paul refers to God's elect people as an "olive tree" in Romans 11:24. The olive tree is made up of Abraham and his seed. But Abraham's seed would only be those who, like Abraham, *believed* God's promise.

This meant that merely being born of the natural seed of Abraham by procreation was not enough to be a part of God's covenant. Only those who *believed* the promise were a part of the olive tree. Therefore being a natural descendant of Abraham did not necessarily mean that they were truly Abraham's children. For example, Abraham had two sons: Ishmael and Isaac. But it was through *Isaac* that Abraham's offspring would be "reckoned" (Gen. 21:12, NIV). In other words, says Paul, "Those who are the children of the flesh are not the children of God, but the children of the promise are counted as descendants" (Rom. 9:8). This is why Paul said that "they are not all Israel who are descended from Israel" (v. 6).

Israelites later became known also as Jews. The gospel was offered to the Jew first (Rom. 1:16). The Jews should have been a part of the natural olive tree. But not all Jews believed the gospel. They forfeited being a part of the true family of God, or what Paul calls the olive tree. The Jews rejecting Jesus resulted in Gentiles being invited to be a part of the olive tree.

The Jews who rejected Jesus are called branches that were "broken off."

This means they are as lost as unbelieving Gentiles are lost. But believing Gentiles, called "a wild olive shoot, were grafted in among them and became a partaker with them of the root and richness of the olive tree" (Rom. 11:17).

This therefore means that there is ultimately no difference between Jew and Gentile: either is saved only by faith in the gospel of Jesus Christ. There is hope for Jews only if they do not persist in unbelief. For God is "able to graft them in again" (v. 23). After all, how much more readily will those, "who are the natural branches, be grafted into their own olive tree?" (v. 24).

This means we as Christians must pray for Israel, witness to Jews, and claim these verses in Romans 11 as a basis for seeing them come to Christ in faith in massive numbers. It is clear that Paul hoped for this. It is my view that the lifting of the blindness presently on Jews—whether in Jerusalem, Tel Aviv, London, Miami Beach, or New York—will be precipitated by the Midnight Cry.

A SLEEPING WORLD

Has not the world always been asleep? Yes. The world, for example, had no knowledge that God sent His Son, made of a woman, to be born in Bethlehem in the "fullness of time" (Gal. 4:4). It happened quietly on a "silent night, holy night" as the Christmas carol puts it. God delights to do things when the world generally is unaware of it.

But there are degrees of sleep, levels of sleep. And I have the conviction that the world is in a deeper sleep than ever—particularly in parts of the world where the gospel once thrived—such as Europe, including Great Britain, and America.

If the church is in a deep, deep sleep, the world is in a deeper sleep. The reason: partly because of the sleeping church. I fear we have ceased to make any impact on the world.

The church is the "salt of the earth" (Matt. 5:13). Jesus said this to His disciples. That means us. We are the salt of the earth. Or at least we are supposed to be. But Jesus immediately added that if the salt loses its saltiness, it is "no longer good for anything" (NIV).

In my book *The Sermon on the Mount* I note five things about salt:

(1) It is an antiseptic. (2) It is makes one thirsty. (3) It is a preservative. (4) It is a seasoning, making things taste better. (5) It is painful to an open wound. These things said, if the church is truly the salt of the earth, it means we will delay decay in this sinful world, our lives will make the world thirsty for what we have, the church will preserve society from getting worse than it is, the church will make the world a happier place, and our gospel will be offensive to a lost world.

It seems to me that the church has lost its saltiness. Instead of delaying decay, we seem to be hastening it. Instead of people wanting what we have, they show no interest. Instead of the church preserving the world—to help keep it from being topsy-turvy—the world is filled with more violence and chaos than ever. Instead of the church helping make the world a safe and happy place, the world is filled with more fear than ever. As for our gospel, generally speaking, what we preach nowadays is not the slightest bit offensive. Instead we are witnessing a great number of teachers saying what people with "itching ears" want to hear rather than what they should hear (2 Tim. 4:3).

COMMON GRACE

The Reformation of the sixteenth century gave us a teaching that is too seldom thought about—the doctrine of common grace. Common grace is God's goodness to all humankind. It is called "common" not because it is ordinary but because it is given commonly to all people. God makes His sun shine and His rain fall on the just and the unjust—the evil and the good (Matt. 5:45). John Calvin called it "special grace in nature." It is what keeps the world from being utterly topsy-turvy. It is what provides law and order—whether through traffic lights or by ordinances to protect society from violence. Common grace is what lies behind the presence of hospitals, doctors, nurses, policemen, and firemen. It is even the explanation for our being born—and where we were born (Acts 17:26). Common grace is a creation gift, this being the explanation for your IQ, your love for music or science, your gifts and talents. It has nothing to do with salvation. It is what comes by virtue of being created in this world.

The world into which we were born is a fallen, sinful world. The world into which the Son of God came is a depraved, wicked world. The church, however, is to be the salt of the earth—part of the reason that the world is no worse than it is, that people are not more evil than they are, that humankind is not more perverse than it is. But if the salt loses its saltiness, the world—depraved though it is—becomes worse than ever.

I fear we have reached that place at the present time. While writing this very section, I stopped for a break and turned on the television. There was an advertisement amidst a political campaign. There were children—aged eight or nine—being scripted to use unprintable foul language against a particular presidential candidate. Such a thing would have been unacceptable and unthinkable only ten years ago!

Michael Youssef has observed how America is the way Israel was in the days of the judges. The era of the judges is summed up: everyone did as he or she saw fit; they all did what was right in their own eyes (Judg. 21:25). The Israelites became tolerant of false gods, complacent, and open-minded toward other religions. This led to Israel cycling through steps in their relationship with God: (1) the people become complacent; (2) they compromise in their beliefs; (3) God moves away because His anger is kindled; (4) He allows His people to fall to oppression; (5) the people call to God for help; (6) God raises up a deliverer. The cycle returns to the first step—complacency—and starts again.[1]

There is more, says Dr. Youssef. Each time this cycle is followed through and begins again, they sink lower and culture has declined a bit further. Each generation that follows this path is more immoral than the generation before. Take the post-World War I era called the "Roaring Twenties," known for its overabundance. Women became increasingly promiscuous, and homosexuality was beginning to be tolerated in media. The Roaring Twenties ended in catastrophe—the financial crash of 1929. When this happened, several repented of their open wickedness, turning to God.[2]

"By any objective standard," says Dr. Youssef, "America in the twenty-first century is a nation in spiritual and moral decline. Many observers date the beginning of American decline to 1962, when the Supreme Court outlawed prayer in public schools. Others date it to 1973, when the Supreme Court legalized unrestricted abortion. These decisions unleashed a tidal wave of harmful effects on our nation—not the least being the estimated fifty-six million human lives destroyed by legal abortion as of 2013."[3]

Dr. Youssef continues: "In 1964, 93 percent of American children were born to married couples. As of 2010, only 59 percent were born in wedlock.... The poverty rate for children in single-parent homes is 37.1 percent, compared with only 6.8 percent in two-parent homes. A child raised by two parents is 82 percent less likely to be in poverty than a child raised by one parent."[4]

This is to say nothing of pornography. Youssef states that in America "12 percent of sites on the Internet are pornographic, 25 percent of Internet searches are requests for pornography, 28,000 Internet users view porn at any given time, 43 percent of all Internet users visit pornographic sites from time to time."[5]

A few years ago when a large number of pastors and church leaders convened in a major city for a conference, they booked most of the hotels in advance. The managers assumed the use of pornographic TV channels would go down to zero. The opposite was the case; orders for the adult channels actually went up—even more than average. This confirms what has been largely reported—that the secret sin of many ministers today is pornography.[6]

Culture is inseparable from common grace. An ever-increasing secular and godless culture has gained ascendancy in America. What was for many years a minority has been overcome by a majority of people—including Christians—becoming impervious to a trend against traditional values. Not long ago I attended a New York Yankees baseball game in Yankee Stadium in Bronx, New York. It has been traditional to hear Kate Smith's rendition of "God Bless America" in the middle of the seventh inning. I ask myself: How long will this continue? I fear that in a short period of time the Yankees management will give in to pressure to drop this tradition.

What is the point of this chapter? The family of God is called the salt of the earth. This means that Christians—brought into God's family by special grace—will have an influence in the world, even influencing the realm of common grace. In a word: if common grace is God's goodness to all men and women, how much more would this special grace in nature be broadened for greater good in the world?

Consider the influence of Great Britain in the world. Why is English spoken around the world, and why does it continue to be the main language used throughout the world? I think it has a lot to do with the Christian heritage of Britain. God has used the English language to advance the gospel. The first modern missionary was William Carey, who was sent to India and planted Christianity there. The influence of Great Britain on the entire world is incalculable. It is because of its Christian heritage. What is called common grace has been more impacting in Great Britain than most countries, even though not all Brits are born again. The family of God is the salt of the earth.

America became the strongest nation in the world. It has continued to send missionaries all over the world. The family of God is the salt of the earth. The fear of God found in its Founding Fathers is the best explanation for the greatness of America.

I am saying that Britain's greatness and America's greatness have in common a Christian heritage. In this way I think either nation can be somewhat compared to Israel. I am certainly *not* supporting the teaching of "British Israel," a point of view that cannot be supported by Scripture. That said, the Judeo-Christian heritage in both nations is not only undeniable but also has contributed to a nation's greatness.

Consider common grace as it has been extended to certain people particularly. What do the following people have in common: Albert Einstein, Henry Kissinger, Benjamin Disraeli, George Gershwin, Leonard Bernstein, Irving Berlin, Groucho Marx, Bob Dylan, Steven Spielberg, Boris Pasternak, Jerome Kern, Martin Buber, Sigmund Freud, and Arthur Rubinstein? They are outstanding Jews. As far as I know, none of them ever came to acknowledge Jesus Christ as their Messiah, and yet these people are extremely talented and demonstrate God's special grace in nature—even if they do not acknowledge this. Irving Berlin's famous song "God Bless America" is an example of the goodness of God through this unusual man. I ask: Would it have occurred to him to write such a song were it not for America's *Christian* heritage? Probably not. I think this suggests that there is a connection between the salt of the earth and the production of great minds and talents in a nation.

But if salt loses its saltiness, what is it good for? It is not good for anything. And I believe something ominous has been developing in Britain and America for a long time: as the Christian influence wanes, so has godlessness in society been on the increase. With godlessness come crime, fear, hate, unbridled sexual promiscuity, and...darkness. The problem today is, I fear, as Bobby Conner once told me, "We have become used to the darkness."

And that is where we are today. Or as I saw Anne Graham Lotz put it on a television show, America has said no to God so often in recent years that God has responded in so many words, "OK. If you don't want Me, I will let you have your nation as you choose." So that is, in my opinion, why we are where we are today.

The church is asleep, and the world is more asleep than ever.

We have become used to the darkness.

CHAPTER 9

THE SUDDEN CRY

At midnight [middle of the night] there was a cry.
—MATTHEW 25:6

I will send My messenger, and he will prepare the way
before Me. And the Lord, whom you seek, will suddenly
come to His temple....But who can endure the day of
his coming, and who can stand when he appears?
—MALACHI 3:1–2

When the day of Pentecost had come...suddenly a sound
like a mighty rushing wind came from heaven.
—ACTS 2:1–2

THE MIDNIGHT CRY WILL COINCIDE WITH A MAJOR CATASTROPHE in the world that will exceed the event of 9/11 in terror, damage, and loss of lives. A word from the messengers—as will be seen below—will come within hours before or after this horrible event. This catastrophe will give great credibility to the message of the messengers. There will also be signs in the heavens at the same time. The prophecy of Joel, which Peter quoted on the Day of Pentecost, included: "I will work wonders in the heavens and the earth—blood and fire and columns of smoke. The sun will be turned to darkness, and the moon to blood, before the great and awe-inspiring day of the LORD comes" (Joel 2:30–31; see also Acts 2:19–20). It is not certain this aspect of Joel's prophecy was visibly fulfilled on the Day of Pentecost. But you can count on this happening during the Midnight Cry. Millions will be shaken rigid from head to toe, falling on their faces, hiding—if possible—from the wrath of the Lamb.

The Midnight Cry will come suddenly, as when the Spirit descended on the Day of Pentecost (Acts 2:2). It will come at a precise moment prior to the second coming of Jesus. As I have been saying, it will come in the middle of the night, metaphorically speaking: it will certainly come in broad daylight for half of the world.

We have seen that the word *midnight* is a translation of three Greek words that mean "middle of the night." At a time when the people of God around the world are in a deep sleep—expecting nothing—there will be a clear word that will be heard around the world. It will be stronger and more widespread in effect than September 11. That word will be a cry—an unmistakable message that will shake the church rigid. It will wake up the church from its long slumber.

The cry will be a word from God, and people will know it is from God. Its content will instantly be recognized as something no man could make up. It will be as clear as the sound of a loud trumpet. It will be a simple, easy-to-understand word that will bring people to their senses in a way no sermon before accomplished. It will not be verbose. It will not be profound. It will not have the ring of a scholar. There will be nothing eloquent about it. It will not appeal to the intellect. It will not play into people's hopes. It will not tickle their ears. It will not be politically correct. It will not favor one's pet theological point of view. It will not appeal to a particular denomination or tradition. It will not play into one's self esteem or feeling of well-being. It will not make people happy. It will not cause instant rejoicing. It will expose our hearts. It will reveal God's verdict of what He thinks of the church. And what He thinks of each of us. It will remove our defensiveness. It will shatter our pride. It will expose our shame. We will accept it whether or not we like it. Many will no doubt be resentful, and yet many will be thankful.

Some awakenings have a gradual beginning; some come suddenly. The New England Awakening came gradually through preaching. It lasted for a generation. The Cane Ridge Revival of 1801 came quite suddenly and lasted only a few days. The Welsh Revival began in a prayer meeting and came suddenly when young Evan Roberts kept praying, "Lord, bend me." The outpouring of the Holy Spirit on the Day of Pentecost was sudden but had followed some ten days of people praying.

The Midnight Cry will be like Pentecost, except that preaching and exhortations will erupt spontaneously, not necessarily in one place and through the preaching of one man, but in many places all over the world by many servants of Christ. Whereas the message of Pentecost was "this is that"—namely Peter explaining the fulfillment of what was foretold by the prophet Joel (Acts 2:16, KJV), the message of the Midnight Cry will be "this is *it*"—namely the fulfillment of what is foretold in Matthew 25:6.

For example, when Jesus read from Isaiah 61:1–2 at the synagogue in Nazareth, He essentially said, "This is *it*." This is what Jesus read:

> The Spirit of the Lord is upon Me, because He has anointed Me to preach the gospel to the poor; He has sent Me to heal the broken-hearted, to preach deliverance to the captives and recovery of sight to the blind, to set at liberty those who are oppressed; to preach the acceptable year of the Lord.
>
> —LUKE 4:18–19

There would have been no uproar had not Jesus immediately added, "*Today* this Scripture is fulfilled in your hearing" (v. 21, emphasis added). That is what was so offensive. It is one thing to say, "The awakening is coming down the road," and people remain in their comfort zones. But when you say, "This is *it*," namely, this *is* the very Midnight Cry Jesus spoke of, it may well strike a chord of violent resentment and anger. That is what happened on the Day of Pentecost; the Midnight Cry will be an elongated wake-up call—lasting months—that will go around the world.

Yes, as we will see in more detail below, thousands and thousands of servants of Christ will take center stage all over the world, focusing on the undoubted certainty of Jesus's soon coming. They will enter into the message that *the coming of the Bridegroom is at hand,* exhorting all the church. The response to Peter's preaching on the Day of Pentecost and the response to the Midnight Cry will be the same: "What shall we do?" (Acts 2:37). Whereas three thousand were cut to the heart by Peter's preaching, millions all over the world will be cut to the heart by spontaneous exhortations—from England to Russia, America to the

Philippines, South Africa to China, and from village to village in every country in the world.

WHAT WILL HAPPEN?

The initial word of the Midnight Cry will be to the church. But this cry will soon address those outside the church. It will spread to those who were previously unreachable—the rich and famous; those who were neglected—the poor and rejected; those who were comfortable and at home with life—the middle class; those who were filled with hate—the racially prejudiced; and those who did not believe in God at all will be shaken in their minds and hearts to their fingertips.

The Greek word for *cry* in Matthew 25:6 is *kraugee*. It is translated "outcry" in Acts 23:9 ("great clamor" in the English Standard Version). It is translated "loud cries" in Hebrews 5:7, a reference to Jesus's praying in Gethsemane. In the ancient Hellenistic world it was used in the sense of proclamation. The Hebrew equivalent was used for crying when calling on God in a national emergency. Its use in Matthew 25:6 shows it was effectual: "Then *all* those virgins rose and trimmed their lamps" (v. 7, emphasis added). The Midnight Cry will be an effectual calling; none of the virgins will sleep through it.

You ask: How will this be heard? What will precipitate this awakening? Will it be like a voice from heaven that the whole world hears simultaneously?

I don't think so. There are *three* categories of the people of God implied in our parable: (1) the wise virgins; (2) the foolish virgins; and (3) the messenger—or, more likely, messengers—who will announce the call. How will they be heard?

I don't know. There are many ways by which God might choose to wake up the church. He could do it with a new movement with thousands of Spirit-filled people in one voice calling the church to wake up. He could do it with a handful—like Gideon's three hundred when God wanted to show what He could do with a small number (Judg. 7:7). He could begin it with one person.

An example of how He might do it would be through smartphones. A specific message could articulate the heart of God in this crucial moment. Smartphones are the main instrument of communication today throughout the world. For example, fifty thousand Muslims rushed to Tahrir Square in Cairo, Egypt, in one hour on January 25, 2011. The vehicle was almost certainly the iPhone. One word did it.

Most young people today don't have a computer. They don't need one. A smartphone gives them all they need—all their communication, news, and connection to the outside world.

It is a small thing for God to come up with a simple word at the right time and moment that will turn the world upside down in hours. I am not saying that a smartphone is the way it will happen; I am only suggesting this as a possibility.

The first Pentecost came about after three years of Jesus's ministry, fifty days after He was raised from the dead, and ten days after His ascension. This meant there were ten days of intense prayer of 120 followers of Jesus prior to the Spirit's outpouring. I have no idea whether there will be an equivalent parallel of intercessory prayer prior to the forthcoming Pentecost. It would not be surprising if a lot of prayer—great prayer meetings, unprecedented intercession by people of God all over the world—would precede the Midnight Cry. I think of ministries like the International House of Prayer as led by Mike Bickle. Movements like these would be a glorious exception to the deep sleep of the church to which I have referred.

You will ask: How much time will elapse between the Midnight Cry and the physical second coming of Jesus? I don't know. I can think of two possibilities: First, my own view, that the second coming of the person of Jesus will follow this wake-up call in a short period of time—say, in a very few years. A lot can happen in even in one or two years: millions of Muslims turning to Jesus Christ, the blindness on Israel lifting—and millions of Jews being saved before the end. This would mean that the bride of Christ has made herself ready in a short period of time, resulting in the glory of the Lord covering the earth as the waters cover the sea. Second, certainly a plausible view, that the time of revival could be lengthened for a good while. Perhaps many years. Either way it will be the knowledge of the glory of the Lord covering the earth "as the waters cover the seas" (Hab. 2:14).

The focus of this book is the fact of the coming Midnight Cry—resulting in the greatest revival in the history of the world.

You will ask: Where will it begin? I don't know. In a sense it doesn't matter, for once the word is out, the entire world will be affected—virtually overnight.

What Can We Do?

You may ask me: If one sincerely believes that the Midnight Cry is coming soon and will precede the second coming, what can Christians do? I answer:

1. Stay alert (Mark 13:37; Luke 12:35).

2. Give all diligence to make sure you have plenty of oil in your lamp by equally pursuing the Word and the Spirit and, regarding the latter, pursue the *fruit* as much as you pursue the *gifts* of the Holy Spirit. The issue of character versus gifting comes into play. And yet surely it is beyond controversy that character is more important than gifting. The gifts are without repentance—irrevocable (Rom. 11:29); there is no need to worry about plenty of oil when it comes to gifts, but this is extremely important when it comes to character.

3. Read the Bible daily with care—I recommend a Bible reading plan that takes you through the entire Bible in a year.

4. Spend as much time in prayer alone with God as you possibly can; I urge thirty minutes a day minimum.

5. Walk in all the light God gives you (1 John 1:7).

6. Be careful to walk in total forgiveness; this means letting all your enemies off the hook and praying that God will bless them.

7. Maintain sexual purity; this means sex only within the bonds of heterosexual marriage.

Doing these seven things will help ensure that you are a wise virgin, not a foolish one.

The Midnight Cry can take place any time. Any day now. I hope this book will serve not merely as a "mini" wake-up call but the means to be ready and looking for this.

I realize that what I am teaching in this book is new to many people. I am presenting what I believe to be true. I utterly sympathize with those who either need time or who will reject it altogether.

Accepting this teaching means a sea change—a paradigm shift—for many readers. Even if you don't accept the thesis of this book, I hope my book will make you want to draw closer to God and make you want to pray more and read your Bible more.

CHAPTER 10

NO CHANGE OF DESTINIES

Then all those virgins rose and trimmed their lamps.
But the foolish said to the wise, "Give us some
of your oil, for our lamps have gone out."
—MATTHEW 25:7–8

For you know that afterward, when [Esau] wanted to inherit
the blessing, he was rejected. For he found no place for
repentance, though he sought it diligently with tears.
—HEBREWS 12:17

ONE OF THE MOST FEARFUL THINGS ABOUT THE MIDNIGHT CRY is that *no destinies are changed* among the ten virgins as a consequence of this wake-up call. The foolish virgins are not given an opportunity to put things right and become wise. Just as the foolish virgins in the parable remained foolish, the wise remained wise. There was no opportunity for repentance. It was too late to change.

Keep in mind that the foolish virgins represent *Christians* who are suddenly exposed as not having enough oil. That means they have not been pursuing their inheritance. They are not granted opportunity for repentance; it is too late for them to become wise.

RECALLING THE OATH

The purpose of this chapter is mainly to explain why it was too late for the foolish virgins to change. It is because of God's oath, a word I explained earlier. In a word, simultaneous with the Midnight Cry is God swearing an oath—in anger. Just as ancient Israel was not able to enter God's rest because He swore an oath concerning them (Heb. 3:11), so the foolish virgins are not able to reverse God's verdict. They will not be granted true repentance. They may well be sorry—or ashamed—that they are found without sufficient oil. But there is nothing they can do about it.

The Midnight Cry will be report card time. The verdict will be in. All will be conscious of God's opinion of their faithfulness—or unfaithfulness—to the Word and Spirit. The wise virgins—those who faithfully pursued the Spirit as well as the Word—will be rewarded. The reward: they go into the wedding banquet (Matt. 25:10). The foolish virgins—those who did not pursue the Holy Spirit—will be shut out of the wedding banquet (vv. 11–12).

When I was a boy in school back in Ashland, Kentucky, I dreaded report card day. My heart would pound in my chest as the teacher handed out the report cards. I dreaded not getting good grades. I hated facing my parents when I got home—especially my dad—with grades that were less than he wanted me to have. The report card told how I had done, this being the teachers' evaluation of my progress. Once the report card was handed out and the results were shown, it was final. I could not change what was written with ink on the card.

What will make the Midnight Cry so fearful is the conscious awareness that we have *God's* verdict. Paul spoke of a coming day when God would step in and reveal His opinion of all of us. "Therefore judge nothing before the appointed time until the Lord comes. He will bring to light the hidden things of darkness and will reveal the purposes of the hearts. Then everyone will have commendation from God" (1 Cor. 4:5). This passage in 1 Corinthians 4:5 is not necessarily a reference to the Midnight Cry, but it nonetheless points to the way God will intervene one day. The Midnight Cry will accomplish this in a sense. Neither is the Midnight Cry the judgment seat of Christ—which comes later, but it will nonetheless cause all Christians to be utterly conscious whether or not they have been faithful in their commitment to the Lord.

"Our lamps have gone out" shows the full awareness that the foolish virgins had of their spiritual state. The saddest thing of all is that repentance for these foolish virgins will not be granted.

Why? It is because behind the Midnight Cry will be God swearing that these people will *not* be allowed into the banquet.

HOW GOD'S OATH COMES INTO PLAY

We dealt with the concept of an oath above. You may wish to reread parts of the chapter in which I dealt with the concept of the oath. God's oath is His irrevocable vow not to change His mind. This is wonderful if God chooses to swear an oath in mercy—as He did to Abraham: "By myself I have sworn, says the LORD, because you have done this thing, and have not withheld your son, your only son, I will indeed bless you and I will indeed multiply your descendants as the stars of the heavens and as the sand that is on the seashore" (Gen. 22:16–17). Abraham never doubted again that God would do this. On previous occasions God made *promises* to Abraham. (See Genesis 12:2–3; 15:5; 17:6–8.) Virtually the same promises would be repeated to keep Abraham encouraged. But when God swore an *oath*, Abraham did not need more promises. They both are equally true and reliable. But promises are generally offered upon conditions. But once the oath is given, there are no conditions; nothing—ever—will change God's mind.

DOES GOD EVER CHANGE HIS MIND?

The complicated theological issue *Does God ever change His mind?* is partly resolved by grasping the difference between the promise and the oath. God might change His mind after giving a promise. Isaiah told Hezekiah that it was time for him to die. Hezekiah wept and pleaded with God, and the same Isaiah came back to Hezekiah with good news: God added fifteen years to his life (2 Kings 20:1–11). Jonah's message to Nineveh was, "In forty days' time, Nineveh will be over-thrown!" (Jon. 3:4). The king of Nineveh called a fast and said, "Who knows? God may relent and change His mind. He may turn from His fierce anger, so that we will not perish" (v. 9). As a result, God had compassion and did not bring the destruction He had threatened (v. 10). John 3:16 is often called the Bible in a nutshell. But it is given on the basis of promise: "For God so loved the world that He gave His only begotten Son, that whoever believes in Him should not perish, but have eternal life." In other words, God loved the world and promised eternal life to those who believe in Him. The gospel is offered on the promise level.

94

So when God communicates at the *promise level*, things might still change: "It ain't over 'til it's over." Someone may stand in the gap and intercede and apparently change God's mind!

But when He swears an oath, *nothing can change His mind.* It was an ancient truism that the oath was irrevocable. It was like the "law of the Medes and Persians, which may not be altered" (Dan. 6:8). An oath was like that. If the oath is given, it's over. Done.

When God swears an oath in wrath—the worst thing possible for any people or persons—it's over. As I mentioned in a previous chapter, this is what happened when the majority of the Israelites outvoted Joshua and Caleb regarding conquering Canaan. Caleb insisted that the Israelites could do it—with the help of God. But no, said the majority: "In our own eyes we were like grasshoppers" (Num. 13:33). The majority ruled.

In that moment God swore in His wrath that no Israelite over the age of twenty would enter the Promised Land (Num. 14:29–30; Heb. 3:10–11). It was over.

And yet the next day the Israelites foolishly decided they were wrong and tried to enter Canaan. Moses warned them not even to *think* about it, that it was too late. They tried anyway and were totally defeated (Num. 14:45). It was *over* before they tried because God swore an oath in wrath. Once the oath is sworn, there will be no change of mind—ever.

This is why it was "impossible" for those Hebrew Christians who had been enlightened, tasted of the heavenly gift, and made partakers of the Holy Spirit to be renewed again to repentance. Repentance was not granted. God swore an oath in wrath concerning certain people. What had they done that was so wrong? Was it immorality? Was it from breaking the Ten Commandments? Possibly not. It was from *not hearing and obeying* God's voice; they eventually became stone deaf to the Holy Spirit. In a word, they came short of their inheritance.

We enter into our inheritance by pursuing both the Word and the Spirit. Those who, after repeated warnings, continue to persist in neglecting what is on offer to them (Heb. 2:3) suffer the horrible consequence of having God swear an oath concerning them.

This is why the writer of the Book of Hebrews warns against being like Esau.

Watching diligently so that no one falls short of the grace of God, lest any root of bitterness spring up to cause trouble, and many become defiled by it, lest there be any sexually immoral or profane person, as Esau, who for one morsel of food sold his birthright. For you know that afterward, when he wanted to inherit the blessing, he was rejected. For he found no place for repentance, though he sought it diligently with tears.

—Hebrews 12:15–17

Whereas the origin of the story of Jacob and Esau demonstrates the sovereignty of God in Jacob being chosen (Gen. 25:23; Rom. 9:10–13), the writer of Hebrews puts the blame squarely on Esau. In any case, Esau could bring about no change of mind. He "found no place for repentance," or rather, "he found no place for a change of mind in his father" (Heb. 12:17, ASV). He could not change what had happened. Behind this episode God had sworn an oath. Esau was sorry, yes, but his sorrow could not undo the fact that Isaac had already given his patriarchal blessing to Jacob (Gen. 27:33).

This is what is so fearful about the Midnight Cry. Once it is uttered, there follows (1) the inescapable universal awareness that Jesus is truly coming soon but (2) the foolish knowing they could not cross over into the wise category. It was absolutely too late for them. They would be kept from the banquet that the wise virgins get to enjoy.

CHAPTER 11

THE MESSAGE

Look, the bridegroom is coming! Come out to meet him!
—MATTHEW 25:6

I am not ashamed of the gospel of Christ. For it is
the power of God for salvation to everyone who
believes, to the Jew first, and also to the Greek.
—ROMANS 1:16

THE MESSAGE OF THE MIDNIGHT CRY WILL COME IN TWO STAGES. The first stage is eschatological and prophetic—that Jesus's second coming is at hand: "Here's the bridegroom! Come out to meet him!" This is what will initially wake up the church. The second stage is soteriological and evangelistic. *Soteriology* refers to the doctrine of salvation. This phase will coincide with the spiritual coming of Jesus, which will soon follow the Midnight Cry. It will mean a clarification of the true gospel combined with evangelism that will go right around the world.

You will recall that the first phase of Jesus's coming is His *spiritual* coming—when power is given to the church as it was in the Book of Acts. This will lead to the bride making herself ready and when the enemies of Jesus become His footstool. It will therefore be a time when the pure gospel—as unfolded in Romans and especially Romans 4—is applied by the Spirit in extraordinary power. This will be the Word and the Spirit coming together: a restoration of the pure gospel with signs and wonders.

The eschatological phase will bring about a succinct message to the church. The word will be prophetic. It will be simple. It will be right to the point. It will be focused. It will be unambiguous. It will be compelling. It will not allow anyone to escape to a place they cannot hear it. No one will be able to hide. For the wake-up call will be effectual. Every

Christian will be instantly sobered and acutely conscious of their spiritual state. There will be sweet relief to the wise virgins, knowing they had been asleep but had oil in their lamps.

Once the church is awakened, the message will enter into a new phase: not only a restoration and clarification of the gospel but also a call to holiness, justice, and a diligent care for the poor; a healing of families, with the hearts of fathers turning to their children; manifestations of signs and wonders; and unprecedented power given for evangelism outside the church.

The initial message of the Midnight Cry to the church, then, will be that Jesus is coming soon. The message outside the church will be the same: Jesus is coming soon.

But why would anyone believe this?

I suspect that the message will burst forth at a moment when the world will be in its greatest turmoil. It will coincide with another major crisis. Two things will make the message of the Midnight Cry believable: (1) the way the message is presented, and (2) conditions in the world at that precise time. Strange as it may seem, the message of the Midnight Cry will be both hated and welcomed.

This message will be accompanied with such power that one of the first realizations of hearers will be that *there really is a God, the Bible is actually true,* and *the same Jesus the Bible talks about is coming again— and soon.* When the message reaches those outside the church, the initial result for some will be not unlike what is described in the Book of Revelation—when poor people, the middle class, royalty, generals, the rich and the powerful, and "everyone, slave and free" will try to hide "from the face of Him who sits on the throne, and from the wrath of the Lamb" (Rev. 6:15–16).

But at the same time millions of people who have not heard the gospel will receive it gladly.

I used to stay at a lovely bed and breakfast place in Northern Ireland. There is a place on a road nearby where there is a sign that cannot be ignored: THE COMING OF THE LORD DRAWETH NIGH. My friend Stephen who drove me to the preaching venue each day said that he can remember seeing this sign when he was a boy—some fifty years before. I suppose people smile when they see this sign from James 5:8 in the King James Version, knowing it has been there for so long and that the Lord's coming has not taken place yet.

It has been a joke for some.

But when the Midnight Cry happens, such a sign will not be something to joke about.

The message of the Midnight Cry therefore will have two phases: (1) when the word "Here's the bridegroom" awakens the church, and (2) when there is an unquestioned restoration of the gospel. This will become an evangelistic message to those outside the church. As it was put in the first generation of the church, God "commands all men everywhere to repent" (Acts 17:30), so too will there be this urgency regarding people's eternal state.

It seems to me that evangelism generally at the present time pays minimal attention to one's eternal state. The emphasis seems to be preponderantly on the "here and now"—what Christianity will do for you *now*. Paul indicated a disdain for preaching like this (1 Cor. 15:19). The next great move of the Holy Spirit will focus on one's eternal state—where you will spend eternity. This is what heightens the importance of being ready for the Midnight Cry as well as the Second Coming.

SIMILARITIES BETWEEN THE CRY AND HIS RETURN

There are three similarities between the Midnight Cry and the physical second coming of Jesus.

First, we do not know the day or the hour of either.

Second, the reaction of people all over the world will be much the same—one of abject dismay but welcomed nonetheless by millions.

Third, people will be literally *wailing* during the immediate fallout of the Midnight Cry as they will be doing when they see Jesus coming in the clouds of glory (Rev. 1:7).

When did you last hear the sound of a wail? A wail is different from weeping or sobbing; it is the sound of pathos—of extreme grief and sorrow; a cry of hopelessness, knowing it is too late. Life as we have known it will change, never to be the same again. The Midnight

Cry will change the world far, far more drastically than any disaster humanity has faced. This is because the message that will be spoken will have lasting power. It will seem as though the coming of the Lord Himself is already taking place. "What shall we do?" is what people will be asking when the Midnight Cry comes.

You may ask: How will this happen? My answer: Once the eschatological phase of the message is heard, thousands and thousands of Christians who have been faithful in their pursuit of the Word and Spirit will take center stage. The cry that the Second Coming is at hand will lead to evangelism and enjoying the banquet. They are invited to the banquet, as we will see below. Not all will be spreading the message of Jesus's soon coming the same way; it will depend on their gifting. As the human body is made up of eyes, ears, hands, feet, and internal organs that are not visible, so the body of Christ is made up of people who are leaders—those with high-profile gifts—but also those who have servant hearts and who work behind the scenes but are as necessary to the body as are kidneys and lungs.

There will be a change in the pecking order of the church; many who had a high profile will be set to one side; their opinions will be irrelevant. And yet many people who have had no profile will become cornerstones in the new era—like the early disciples who startled the religious leaders: "illiterate and uneducated" people whose qualifications were "that they had been with Jesus" (Acts 4:13).

Therefore as John the Baptist was the forerunner of the public ministry of Jesus, so will the Midnight Cry be the forerunner of the second coming of Jesus. As John the Baptist ministered in the spirit and power of Elijah (Luke 1:17), so will there be many John the Baptists who will confront enemies of the gospel as Elijah himself did on Mount Carmel (1 Kings 18:16–40). Those church leaders—pastors, teachers, and evangelists in the church—some high profile, some otherwise—who have been true and faithful to the Word and the Holy Spirit will have a greater ministry than ever. But those who have replaced the gospel with a compromised message will fade away. Those who have been ashamed of the gospel, including those who cater to people with itching ears and give false hopes of prosperity, will be humiliated overnight and made null and void. To the latter it will be like Jesus overthrowing the moneychangers in the temple (John 2:14–16). This will not be a time of joy for the false teachers and prophets of this world or those who use the Bible to cater to the worldly passions of people.

These things said, the second phase of the Midnight Cry will result in millions from all over the world being saved in a very short period of time. It will be like the amazing success of King Hezekiah. "Hezekiah and all the people rejoiced that God had prepared the people, since *the events happened suddenly*" (2 Chron. 29:36, emphasis added). Millions and millions of Muslims will be converted in months. This will affect the Jews too. Paul hoped that the conversion of Gentiles would provoke Israel to jealousy (Rom. 11:11).

ROMANS 4

I would like to elaborate on the previously mentioned vision of John Paul Jackson. Several years before he died, John Paul was given a glimpse of what I am describing in this chapter. In a vision there came a messenger of God who announced the coming move of God on the earth, and added: "The key to the next great move of God on the earth is found in the Book of Romans and especially chapter 4."[1] This messenger stated that certain Christian leaders had violated the Romans 4 principle. These would lose their ministries and some would die. But those who had not violated the Romans 4 principle would one day suddenly be placed "where no one has stood since the days of the early church." This meant a restoration of the gospel and authentic manifestations of healing, signs, and wonders. I will say more about this below.

The Romans 4 principle is two things, and Abraham is the example of each. First, it is a restoration of the teaching of justification by faith alone, believing the promise as Abraham did (Rom. 4:1–11). Second, it is pursuing one's inheritance as Abraham did, namely, believing that Isaac would be born despite his and Sarah's age (vv. 12–21).

Surprising as it may seem, the message that *Jesus is coming soon* is what will get the world's attention, but the same gospel as outlined by Paul in Romans—and no doubt all his letters—is what will be the theological content of evangelism. Moreover, the church will demonstrate holiness, true justice, and care for the poor. As John the Baptist's message began with a warning to flee from the wrath to come but also called for bearing fruit "worthy of repentance" (Luke 3:8), so will the church be instrumental in spreading social justice in the land, as John the Baptist also called for (vv. 11–15). All this will be a part of the bride of Christ making herself ready for Jesus's coming.

CHAPTER 12

THE MESSENGERS

At midnight there was a cry, "Look, the bridegroom
is coming! Come out to meet him!"
—MATTHEW 25:6

The voice of one crying in the wilderness: "Prepare
the way of the Lord; make His paths straight."
—MATTHEW 3:3

YOU WILL RECALL THAT THERE ARE THREE CATEGORIES OF Christians implied in the parable of the ten virgins: (1) the wise virgins, (2) the foolish virgins, and (3) the messengers—those who wake up the church in the middle of the night, metaphorically speaking.

As we saw above, the role of the messengers comes into play when they are given a message at the time a major catastrophe takes place somewhere in the world. It will shake not just one part of the world but the entire world. But with that catastrophe will be the *message of the messengers.* Coming almost simultaneously with the world-shaking event itself will be a *word—a clear and simple word—*that will be as traumatic as the catastrophe itself.

Who then will be bringing this Cry in the middle of the night? Is it an angel? Will it be one of the superstars we see on religious TV? The answer is, it will be chosen vessels who have a John the Baptist type of ministry.

There was only one John the Baptist to precede the ministry of Jesus Christ. But there will be many John the Baptists to precede the second coming of Jesus. Certain people will have a John the Baptist type of ministry.

It could, of course, be one person who announces the soon coming of Jesus. But it will actually be many who participate in the Midnight

Cry. The "cry" that will ring out will be carried out by sovereign vessels. Sovereign vessels are God's servants chosen by Him for a specific mission. Those people described in Hebrews 11 *who by faith* accomplished what they did were sovereign vessels. Those living today who succeed and follow in the steps of those in Hebrews 11 will be signally used to wake up the church and the world.

As I observed above, this therefore shows that there are *three* categories of people who are described in the parable of the ten virgins: (1) the wise virgins—who took oil in their lamps; (2) the foolish virgins—who took no extra oil in their lamps; and (3) those who actually *announce* the Midnight Cry.

Not all Christians—not even those wise virgins who come into their inheritance—are necessarily sovereign vessels. One does not have to be like those described in Hebrews 11 to be a wise virgin. The wise and foolish virgins are those people of God who have professed faith in His name and believed the gospel. But they may not be extraordinary like those in Hebrews 11. Those in Hebrews 11 are prime examples of sovereign vessels.

To put it another way: as we have seen, not all Christians come into their inheritance. Those who don't are called foolish virgins in the parable of the ten virgins. Those who do come into their inheritance are called wise virgins in this parable. And yet, as I said, not all the wise virgins are necessarily sovereign vessels. Sovereign vessels are those who have an unusual, even lofty, calling. I will not enter into the discussion whether those who carry out the Midnight Cry are apostolic or prophetic ministers or teachers. Perhaps they are all of these. They are certainly *evangelists*. But probably not superstars. They will come out of nowhere—like Elijah the Tishbite (1 Kings 17:1). They will possibly be not highly educated—like the early disciples (Acts 4:13). They will have been preserved like Joseph waiting for his time to come (Gen. 41:38–44). Some will have been prepared like Moses (Acts 7:22–23), some like Samuel (1 Sam. 3:19–20), and some like Daniel (Dan. 1:8). Whether a person with the apostle Paul's intellect will be needed during this time, I don't know. The earliest church immediately after Pentecost did not include great theologians.

You will recall the previously mentioned vision given to the late John Paul Jackson when the messenger of God announced that the key to the next move of God on the earth would be the Book of Romans and especially Romans chapter 4. John Paul saw more in this vision. A group of men took their seats on three of four rows of bleachers—seats without backs. The messenger of God had a word for the men seated on the third row: "You men on the third row have abused the Romans 4 principle. Some of you will live, some of you will die, but none of you will succeed no matter how hard you try."[1] He then had a word for those on the first and second rows: "You men on rows one and two have not abused the Romans 4 principle. On a day you least expect you will be catapulted to the fourth row where no man has stood since the days of the early church."

That is the end of John Paul's vision. He had the vision in 1986. He related it to me in 2001. I discussed this with him several times before he died. He wanted to emphasize that the catapulting of those men on rows one and two to the fourth row represented "a new pecking order." Those on row three had rather high profiles at one time. They had lorded their ministries over those in rows one and two. He even recognized certain men on the third row—those who were said to have abused the Romans 4 principle. What John Paul saw in these men turned out exactly as was stated. Some had been household names. I would call them "yesterday's men." Some of them have tried and tried and tried to come back to their previous stature, usefulness, and profile, but they have failed.

This also suggests that these men came short of their inheritance, that is, by abusing the Romans 4 principle. Such people were saved but tragically brought disgrace upon the name of Christ—whether through sexual sin, misuse of money, or lust for power and personal glory.

A man I respect deeply shared with me the following story. He has intimate experiences with the Holy Spirit. He is no "flake"; he is a serious man whose ministry all over the world—especially to China—has made a huge impact. He was praying one day, asking the Lord: "Am I a wise virgin?"

The reply: "No."

He was shocked and then asked the Lord: "Then am I a foolish virgin?"

The reply: "No."

Puzzled by this, he asked the Lord again: "Am I a wise virgin?"

"No."

"Then I must be a foolish virgin."

"No." Then the Lord said to him that there will be a third category of believers—a remnant of those in the church who are *awake and not asleep*. They will be among those who *carry out* the Midnight Cry. They will be the instruments God uses to wake up the church.

The messengers of the Midnight Cry will be sovereign vessels who turn out to be worthy of their calling. They will be sexually pure. They will not be motivated by the praise of people. They will not be influenced by the love of money. They will be those who break the betrayal barrier, a concept I will explain in part 3 of this book.

Those who are the messengers of the Midnight Cry, unlike the ten virgins, will be *awake and expectant.*

The bride of Christ is not mentioned in the parable of the ten virgins. The ten virgins are not intended to refer to the bride of Christ but rather to describe what is typical of the church today. And yet the parable indicates three categories of people in Christ's bride: (1) those sleeping virgins who nonetheless pursued the Word and the Spirit—the wise; (2) those sleeping virgins who did not carefully pursue the Word and the Spirit—the foolish; and (3) those servants of Christ in the church who have stayed awake—the messengers of the Midnight Cry.

Are you truly *awake*? Be sobered. You may be one of God's messengers who have come to the kingdom for such a time as this.

CHAPTER 13

THE AWAKENED CHURCH

Then all those virgins rose and trimmed their lamps.
—MATTHEW 25:7

Then I heard something like the sound like a great multitude, as
the sound of many waters and as the sound of mighty thunderings,
saying: "Alleluia! For the Lord God Omnipotent reigns! Let us
be glad and rejoice and give Him glory, for the marriage of the
Lamb has come, and His wife has made herself ready. It was
granted her to be arrayed in fine linen, clean and white."
—REVELATION 19:6–8

WHAT WILL THE CHURCH BE LIKE AFTER THE MIDNIGHT CRY?
The purpose of this chapter is an attempt to answer that
question.

The words *revival* and *awakening* are often used interchangeably.
Since this is partly a matter of semantics, we should not press the distinction too far. But one might argue that revival refers to Christians
being revived and that awakening refers to the community outside the
church being shaken. And yet sometimes the church itself needs to be
awakened, and that is what the parable of the ten virgins is partly about.
The ten virgins refer to the church. But as the bride is not mentioned
in the parable of the ten virgins, we must remember the principle that a
parable does not stand evenly on all four legs.

THE CHURCH IS THE BRIDE OF CHRIST

The church is depicted as a bride in at least four places in the New
Testament. John the Baptist may have been the first to teach this: "He
who has the bride is the bridegroom. But the friend of the bridegroom,

who stands and hears him, rejoices greatly at the bridegroom's voice" (John 3:29).

Second, Paul said, "Husbands, love your wives, just as Christ also loved the church and gave Himself for it, that He might sanctify and cleanse it with the washing of water by the word, and that He might present to Himself a glorious church, not having spot, or wrinkle, or any such thing, but that it should be holy and without blemish" (Eph. 5:25–27).

And though Paul presses the practical issue of a husband loving his wife as Christ loved the church, he concludes that section by saying: "This is a great mystery, but I am speaking about Christ and the church" (v. 32). These lines clearly imply that the church is seen as the bride of Christ.

Third, Paul wrote to the Corinthians: "For I am jealous over you with godly jealousy. For I have espoused you to one husband, that I may present you as a chaste virgin to Christ" (2 Cor. 11:2).

Fourth, when John records these words, "For the marriage of the Lamb has come, and His wife has made herself ready" (Rev. 19:7), it is clear that the church is to be seen as Christ's bride. But Jesus is still physically at the right hand of God when this happens. And yet the wedding itself, though it is at hand, does not take place yet. The bride is "ready." This means that the church has at long last become what God wanted it to be—pure like a virgin. The actual wedding takes place later in God's scheme (Rev. 21:1–4).

The point here is this: although the church has been asleep and part of the church is described as foolish virgins, the wise virgins who are invited to the wedding banquet fulfill the ultimate purpose of God regarding the church. The wise virgins—namely those who were "ready" (Matt. 25:10)—demonstrate the kind of church God has willed.

THE FEAR OF GOD WILL
RETURN TO THE CHURCH

When the church is revived, it means that Christians will become more like what they ought to have been all along. When the church is what it ought to be, the world will begin to respect the church.

Sadly, the world does not respect the church as I write these lines. Mary Queen of Scots (1542–1587) is reported to have said that she feared the prayers of John Knox (c. 1514–1572) more than all the armies of Europe.[1] But who respects the church today? Virtually no one. The world laughs at us. They see us as a big joke. No one is afraid of us. Turn on typical Christian television, and it is all about money, feeling good, and "What's in it for me?" But there is virtually no fear of God.

The Midnight Cry will result in an immediate fear of God—in the church and the world.

But should the world be afraid of the church? Yes. The world should fear the church. This means the world should be very, very respectful of it. In the earliest church those outside it stepped to one side with deepest respect when the believers in Christ were around. The early church met in Solomon's Porch, part of the ancient temple. "No one else dared join them, but the people respected them" (Acts 5:13). This means that the non-believing Jews knew their place when around these believers. They showed a very deep respect for those who believed that Jesus was the Messiah. Why? It is because a fear of God settled on all. An awakened church will gain the world's respect for it. When Jacob, having been in a backslidden state, got right with God (Gen. 35:1–4), "the terror of God was on *the cities that were around them, and they did not pursue the sons of Jacob*" (v. 5, emphasis added).

In our parable the foolish and wise virgins were *all* awakened. After the middle-of-the-night Cry "all those virgins rose and trimmed their lamps" (Mt. 25:7). The Cry indicated that the Bridegroom's coming was finally at hand. And all believed it. One of the most extraordinary things about the Midnight Cry will be that the entire church throughout the world will be convinced that the coming of Jesus is truly at hand. The church's awakening will spill over into communities outside the church.

As we will see below, *evangelism* will have top priority. Instead of endless introspection and Christians chasing after a "feel good" state of mind, the church will turn to the lost outside it. What will impel the church to evangelize will be the consciousness of God's coming judgment on unbelievers.

You will recall that an animated conversation followed between the foolish and the wise virgins (Matt. 25:8–9). This is partly because the second coming of Jesus—Jesus leaving His throne at the right hand of God—was at hand but had not yet arrived. It was a time for the church to get ready for the second coming and for those outside the church to get ready for it. The message will be that the Bridegroom's coming is at hand indeed, but there is still a degree of time. For one thing, the wise would repent of being asleep. And although it was too late, the foolish would plead with the wise for spiritual help.

Picture this. Those in the church who had been on the periphery of the life of the church suddenly pleading tearfully with the faithful: "Pray for us. Please pray for us." The reply will be: "We wish we could help. We have barely enough grace for ourselves."

But foolish virgins will not only be comprised of those on the periphery; it will include those thought to be stalwarts! People like this become smug and, sadly, out of touch with communion of the Spirit. They too will be among those who plead with the wise, "Give us some of your oil." But it will be too late.

The door will be shut. There is no way that the foolish virgins can have a part in this great revival. This is one of the ways "weeping and gnashing of teeth" can be applied to those in the church. They will realize what they have missed.

In the meantime, the Bridegroom will come. We will see further below that the coming of the Bridegroom initially means the coming of the Spirit in power. The wise virgins—those who are "ready"—will go into the wedding banquet. The foolish virgins will appeal to the door-keeper for entrance into the celebration. "Open the door for us!" they will plead. "I do not know you," the doorkeeper will tell them (Matt. 25:11–12).

TEN THINGS THAT WILL CHARACTERIZE AN AWAKENED CHURCH

1. The gospel restored

It makes perfect sense that the Book of Romans, and especially Romans 4, will be the key to this great move of the Holy Spirit. Romans was the key New Testament book in the time of the Protestant

Reformation. Romans 4 is Paul's expounding of justification by faith alone—the central teaching of the Reformation. The world was turned upside down by this teaching. The same exact message is what led to John Wesley's conversion—when his heart was "strangely warmed" at Aldersgate Street in London in 1738.[2] This led him to preach it all over England for the next generation. It was the message of Jonathan Edwards in Northampton, Massachusetts, from 1735–1740 that led to the Great Awakening in New England. It is not the purpose of my book to enter into the minute details of all I believe about the gospel—only to say two things: (1) the same gospel of Paul, Luther, Edwards, and Wesley will be revived and upheld with an unashamed command for people everywhere to be saved by faith in the blood of Christ propitiating the justice of God the Father, and (2) there will be a return to the preaching of the eternal wrath of God.

2. Holiness

Holy living—a care to please God by financial integrity, sexual purity, a demonstration of the fruit of the Holy Spirit, and a desire to glorify God in the whole of one's personal life—will become the norm. This will mean a restoration of Christian marriage between a man and a woman—and couples living in faithfulness to one another. People living in homosexual practice will be convicted by the Holy Spirit that they are in sin and will volunteer to honor the clear teaching of Holy Scripture. A return to unfeigned care for the family will be widespread throughout the world. The fruit of the Spirit—love, joy, peace, patience, goodness, gentleness, faith, meekness, and self-control—will be sought after for Christian character.

We saw earlier in the book that one of the things about sleep is that we do things in our sleep we would not do when awake. When the church is awakened by the Midnight Cry, there will be deep repentance in the church all over the world for the way we have lived—as if in a dreamlike state. We will be shocked over the kind of lives we lived and how we tolerated the things that no longer gave us a sense of outrage. We will repent of such and aspire to living holy lives—as we should have been doing. May I remind you, I want my book to be a mini wake-up call—a drop in the bucket to what is coming down the road.

3. Priority of family life

Malachi prophesied, "See, I will send you Elijah the prophet before the coming of the great and dreaded day of the LORD. He will turn the hearts of the fathers to their children, and the hearts of the children to their fathers" (Mal. 4:5–6). The angel Gabriel prophesied that John the Baptist would go forth "in the spirit and power of Elijah, to turn the hearts of the fathers to the children and the disobedient to the wisdom of the just, to make ready a people prepared for the Lord" (Luke 1:17).

Possibly the saddest fact of our generation is the utter disintegration of the family unit. Fathers in particular have abdicated their parental responsibility in America and Britain. The result is unprecedented numbers of single parents—mostly mothers—having to bring up their children. Many children growing up today have no relationship with their fathers. This is a recipe for lack of sexual identity later in life. Some have no idea who their father is because sometimes the mother is not sure. But there will be a great sense of repentance coming to parents after the Midnight Cry, restoring families and bringing dads home to love their children.

4. The return of millions of young people to the church

The generation gap that has developed so sharply in the last fifty years in the church—resulting in more and more young people leaving it—will be more and more closed as a result of the Midnight Cry and the spiritual coming of Jesus. The restoration of parents and children not only means a return to focus on the family; it also means the return of young people to the church.

We have been losing countless numbers of young people in recent years. There are various explanations for this—boring church services, boring sermons, or lack of connection between the church's message and the real world. The main reason for the loss of young people is that they do not see the Christian message as relevant or true. The Midnight Cry will change that overnight. Many, many young people—teenagers and those in their twenties and thirties—will flock to the church in earnest haste; in anxiety, desperation, and heart-searching. The spiritual coming of Jesus will fill the need.

5. The working class and ordinary people leading the way in number of people converted

Dr. Martyn Lloyd-Jones used to say to me, "Christianity has not touched the working class in Britain." Those words gave me pause. He is so right. When I was at Westminster Chapel, we tried to reach all classes of people but had only modest success. It was the middle class who came to the chapel by and large. The same is true in America. Whether it be Southern Baptists, Presbyterians, or Pentecostals, Christianity has appealed largely to the middle class. And yet in the New Testament it is said of Jesus: "The common people heard him gladly" (Mark 12:37, KJV). Not only that, but Paul also made it painfully clear that God's elect are largely chosen from ordinary people: "Among you, not many wise men according to the flesh, not many mighty men, and not many noble men were called. But God has chosen the foolish things of the world to confound the wise. God has chosen the weak things of the world to confound the things which are mighty. And God has chosen the base things of the world and things which are despised" (1 Cor. 1:26–28). The next great move of God will reach the poor, the rejected, the homeless, the uneducated, and the jobless. No one will feel left out. Because Jesus left no one out.

6. Concern for the poor and the "underdog"

Evangelicals' uneasy conscience for neglecting the "poor" of James 2:6, for example, will lead the church to show their faith by "good works"—not merely saying "God bless you" but by active involvement for hurting people (vv. 14–17). "Religion that is pure and undefiled before God, the Father, is this: to visit the fatherless and widows in their affliction and to keep oneself unstained by the world" (James 1:27). An awakened church will no longer sweep the dirt under the carpet by showing disdain for the underprivileged and the unemployed but will show compassion not unlike that of the William Booths of this world. This will be a part of the bride making herself ready.

7. Evangelism

I do not anticipate organized mass evangelistic campaigns but rather many Christians doing the work of an evangelist. Although we will need the leadership of high-profile evangelists, I predict that there will be few superstars. I expect the evangelism to be spontaneous, as it was when Philip approached the Ethiopian (Acts 8:26–36) or when Peter took advantage of the platform provided by the healing of the man by the gate of the temple called Beautiful (Acts 3:1–20).

This is to say nothing of the power of the Holy Spirit falling all over the church throughout the world at the onset of the Midnight Cry— with countless people being saved because they cry out to God in Jesus's name. As we will see further below, Muslims will be open to the gospel. Thousands of people—including imams—who have had dreams that Jesus was the Son of God and died on a cross will surface and openly turn to Jesus Christ. As we will see further below, Muslims turning to Christ in mass numbers will be a part of what will awaken the conscience of Jews all over the world. Truly, the glory of the Lord will cover the earth as the waters cover the sea. Indeed, the angel Gabriel stated that John the Baptist would bring many of the people of *Israel* back to the Lord their God (Luke 1:16). Do not forget: the Midnight Cry will result in a John the Baptist ministry to the church.

8. Church unity

The first Pentecost came when the disciples were of one accord (Acts 2:1, KJV). This was without doubt an essential ingredient in the initial coming of the Spirit to the church. Jesus prayed for church unity in John 17:21, that the church may be "one." This too will be a vital factor in the bride making herself ready for the coming of the Lord.

Instead of Christians pointing the finger at each other and churches competing with each other, the awakening will convict all of us of our selfishness and having a rival spirit. The Midnight Cry will bring about true fellowship with all Christians; instead of a prevalence of suspicion toward those who don't see eye to eye with us, there will be a love for one another—an overlooking of nonessentials. At the height of the Cane Ridge Revival the issues that had divided churches—the issue of baptism, the nuances of church government, and even the nuances that had divided Calvinists and Arminians—became irrelevant. That is, until the revival was over and churches sadly returned to arguing and debates.

But the coming movement of the Spirit will bring a beautiful church unity—a great part of the bride making herself ready.

9. Signs and wonders

Apart from multitudinous conversions, many people will be healed. Signs and wonders—including people like Ananias and Sapphira being struck dead (Acts 5:1–11)—can be expected after the Midnight Cry.

I am sure that there have been many Ananiases and Sapphiras of this world over the centuries who have lied to the Spirit but have not been suddenly taken home to heaven. Why not? I think it is because we have not been in a revival situation. But this will change after the Midnight Cry.

The fact of holiness generally being the norm in the church would not mean that anyone is sinless. But I fully expect the blind to be healed, even hospitals sometimes to be emptied and the dead to be raised—just to demonstrate the power of the ascended Christ before He makes all His enemies His footstool.

10. Many backsliders restored

A vital part of the John the Baptist ministry was that he would "turn many of the sons of Israel to the Lord their God" (Luke 1:16). This verse in Luke could mean more than one thing. First, in the original context it would refer to those within Israel—the household of faith—who are backslidden but get restored. This no doubt happened when John preached "repentance" (Luke 3:8). Thousands came back to a right relationship with God through John's ministry.

Second, I would anticipate this to happen in the coming awakening. There are many who made professions of faith but deserted the church. A John the Baptist ministry will touch people like that. Many backsliders will return to the church.

If someone asks, "Why cannot this apply to the foolish virgins? Were they not backsliders too?," I reply: the foolish virgins were in a category that describes those who could not be restored to repentance, as in Hebrews 6:4–6. It is not easy to draw the line between foolish virgins in the church who cannot be restored and backsliders in the world who may be restored.

I would only suggest that the foolish virgins were *not* like those who had not gone back into the world but were like the Laodiceans—smug, who "have need of nothing" (Rev. 3:17). Jesus said there were prostitutes who believed John the Baptist, and people like them enter the kingdom of God before Pharisees (Matt. 21:31–32). The foolish virgins were more like Pharisees—self-righteous, judgmental, and unteachable—that is, until it was too late for them.

Third, as John the Baptist brought many "of the people of *Israel*" back to the Lord, so would the Midnight Cry do this for modern Israel. This would mean Jews *today—anywhere in the world*. The coming revival will result in the lifting of the blindness on Israel, as we have seen. Therefore the John the Baptist type of ministry that precedes the physical second coming of Jesus will play a huge part in the restoration of Israel in the very last days.

REACHING THE UNREACHABLE

We saw above that the gospel will be effectual mostly with those who are not exactly the aristocracy of this world. Paul said that not many mighty or noble are called, but God has called the ordinary people of this world (1 Cor. 1:26–27). But there will be those, nonetheless, who were previously unreachable—like people in the Mafia, politicians, heads of state, the wealthy, and the famous—who will come out of hiding to profess openly their faith in Christ. Not many. The Nicodemuses and the Josephs of Arimathea are rare. But there will be some. And the "some" will make world news.

The media

Imagine what this will do to newspaper headlines. The Welsh Revival made second-page news day after day in Wales. I have read original editions of Welsh newspapers that give a daily report of what happened in various churches the day before. The Midnight Cry will make front-page news in all newspapers of the world. The media will not be able to ignore the next and final great move of God.

World news

Apart from the next great move of God being world news, its effect will be widespread in the Middle East and all nations. What a difference in Iraq, Iran, Egypt, Syria, and Saudi Arabia! With millions of Muslims being saved from Indonesia to Pakistan, the entire political climate of the world will change. If the Welsh Revival resulted in jails being largely empty, how much more will corruption be lessened in the nations and cities where this revival permeates—whether Russia or New York, China or London. China is already set to be the leading Christian nation of the world; the coming move of God will more than complete this expectation, resulting in countless millions of Chinese people coming to Christ.

As was mentioned previously, Jesus said that the church is the salt of the earth (Matt. 5:13). Salt among other things is a seasoning. This suggests that the church will have an effect in the world but not that the whole world will be saved. The next great move of God will not save everybody. But the world will not be the same.

Isaac is coming.

CHAPTER 14

THE COMING OF
THE BRIDEGROOM

While they went to buy some [oil], the bridegroom came.
—Matthew 25:10

I saw heaven opened. And there was a white horse. He who sat on
it is called Faithful and True, and in righteousness He judges and
wages war. His eyes are like a flame of fire, and on His head are many
crowns. He has a name written, that no one knows but He Himself.
He is clothed with a robe dipped in blood. His name is called The
Word of God. The armies in heaven, clothed in fine linen, white and
clean, followed Him on white horses. Out of His mouth proceeds a
sharp sword, with which He may strike the nations. "He shall rule
them with an iron scepter." He treads the winepress of the fury and
wrath of God the Almighty. On His robe and on His thigh He has
a name written: KING OF KING AND LORD OF LORDS.
—Revelation 19:11–16

T HE ABOVE PASSAGE IN REVELATION REFERS TO THE *SPIRITUAL*
coming of Jesus, not when He personally and physically leaves
His throne at the Father's right hand. This point of view is not the position of many of my friends who take this passage to refer to the physical
second coming of Jesus.

I used to believe that the above passage in Revelation 19 referred to
the physical, personal second coming of Jesus and that it comes seven
years after the "rapture" of the church. According to this view, the
saved—the church—are suddenly "caught up" to meet the Lord in the
air, as put by Paul in 1 Thessalonians 4:17. These are the redeemed who
are not only taken to heaven, but they are also saved from the great tribulation that instantly follows. According to this view, chapters 4–19 of

Revelation describe events that take place over a period of seven years. Those who hold to this see the rapture described in Revelation 4:1. They are called "pretribulation premillennialists." This means that the second coming is in two phases: (1) the rapture and (2) the revelation of Christ as He comes visibly from heaven to defeat His enemies. Then comes the thousand-year reign—called the millennium. These views are called "pretrib" because the rapture of the church takes place *before* the great tribulation. At the end of seven years, say these interpreters, Jesus literally and personally comes, and this is what is meant in Revelation 19:11ff. However, there are those who believe that the rapture comes in the middle of the seven-year period. They are called "midtrib" premillennialists. And yet some believe the second coming takes place at the end of the seven-year period and are called "posttrib" premillennialists. All three of these views are consistent with premillennialism. I was taught the "pretrib" perspective from my pastor in Ashland, Kentucky. Following the Scofield Reference Bible and the charts of Clarence Larkin, I embraced this. By the time I was eighteen years old, I had a firm grasp of this teaching. When I was a student at Trevecca Nazarene University, I actually was invited to teach the Book of Revelation by our New Testament professor! Yes—aged eighteen and I knew it all! It has taken more than sixty years for me to come to the position taken in the book you are now reading.

You will recall my own view that the second coming is to be grasped as being in two stages: (1) the spiritual coming; that is, Jesus sending the Spirit in power—the Midnight Cry; and (2) the physical coming, when Jesus personally leaves His place at the right hand of God. The first phase of the arrival of the Bridegroom is what I believe is described above in Revelation 19. It describes the *spiritual* coming of Christ—what Jesus does from the Father's right hand through the power of the Spirit.

Revelation 19:11–16 is therefore not a description of the personal, physical return of Jesus, as I used to think, but the spiritual, triumphant coming of Jesus when He defeats His enemies by the Word of God. This happens soon after the wake-up call while the foolish virgins were trying to get oil. They were pleading with the wise virgins to give them oil. But it was too late for them. They would forfeit getting to enjoy the greatest move of the Holy Spirit since Pentecost.

The essential difference between my view and most premillennialists is that I believe Jesus defeats His enemies from the right hand of the Father—without leaving His throne. The latter believe He leaves His throne and then defeats His enemies. But because of the claim He would not leave His throne until He makes His enemies His footstool, I take the view as put in this book.

The passage in Revelation 19:11–16 is therefore a description of the great revival that follows the wake-up call. This is how King Jesus—orchestrating the move of the Holy Spirit from the right hand of God—defeats His enemies. It is by the Word and the Spirit. "Out of His mouth proceeds a sharp sword, with which He may strike the *nations*" (Rev. 19:15, emphasis added). The *Word* will do it. Evangelists will do it. The wise virgins will be right in the middle of it. They may not be superstars. It will be, as I said, by and large, carried out by ordinary Christians who have a gift of evangelism. God may well use the J. Johns and Billy Grahams of this world. But the thrust of this movement will be God's chosen and empowered ordinary people who propagate the gospel by the authority and power of the Holy Spirit.

Some think that this kind of victory can only be achieved by Jesus Himself personally leaving His throne in heaven and coming to the earth to defeat His enemies—whether Islam or unregenerate Judaism. Wrong. He will do it without leaving His throne. He will *not* leave His throne until He makes all His enemies His footstool (Ps. 110:1; 1 Cor. 15:25).

Which do you suppose brings greater glory to God: Jesus personally and physically coming to the earth to overcome His enemies or Jesus doing it from the right hand of God? The answer is, He will gain more glory by doing it in heaven—using His servants—the wise virgins!

To put it another way, it would be *easy* for Jesus to defeat His enemies by His physical return to the earth! But the challenge of challenges will be when God uses people like *you and me*—while Jesus personally stays in heaven!

The Spiritual Coming of Jesus

The purpose of this chapter is to explain more of this spiritual coming of Jesus as described by John in Revelation 19:11–19. The passage in Revelation demonstrates how effectual the *spiritual* coming of the Lord will be—using ordinary people to do His work.

The parable merely states that "the bridegroom came" (Matt. 25:10). Nothing more is said. It is here that another intentional ambiguity comes into play in the parable of the ten virgins. The arrival of the bridegroom certainly refers to second coming of Jesus. And yet our parable only demonstrates the fallout of the *spiritual* coming of Jesus for the five foolish and five wise virgins.

The arrival of the bridegroom thus means the twofold sense of the second coming. Jesus adds no eschatological details to this in the parable. For example, no mention is made of His coming with glory and the holy angels, no mention is made of clouds, and—most importantly—no mention is made of the resurrection of the dead. This shows that the arrival of the bridegroom in the parable is the spiritual coming of Jesus prior to the physical coming.

Indeed, what follows in the parable can only be described as activities that precede the physical coming of the Lord Jesus. The focus is on the foolish virgins trying desperately to get into the wedding banquet. The foolish virgins will be shut out. Only the wise virgins are invited to the wedding banquet.

A wedding banquet *precedes* a marriage being consummated—it doesn't follow. To put it another way, the wedding banquet comes before the "honeymoon"—not after. Not only that; the bride is not mentioned at all in the parable. This is because the actual marriage takes place after the physical coming of Jesus. The absence of a mention of the bride therefore further illustrates that the actual marriage takes place *after* the events described in Matthew 25:10–13:

> But while they went to buy some, the bridegroom came, and those who were ready went in with him to the wedding banquet. And the door was shut. Afterward, the other virgins came also, saying, "Lord, Lord, open the door for us."

But he answered, "Truly I say to you, I do not know you." Watch therefore, for you know neither the day nor the hour in which the Son of Man is coming.

The reference to the "wedding banquet" points directly to the "marriage supper" in Revelation 19:7–9: "For the marriage of the Lamb has come, and His wife has made herself ready. It was granted her to be arrayed in fine linen, clean and white.... Blessed are those who are invited to the marriage supper of the Lamb."

THE WISE VIRGINS
TAKE CENTER STAGE

The event described in Revelation 19 demonstrates how the King of kings makes His enemies His footstool—all from the throne of God. He does this by remote control, as it were, namely by the power of the Word of God and enabling of the Spirit. Those wise virgins who had been faithful in pursuing the Word and the Spirit now take center stage in the greatest revival in the history of the church. The foolish virgins do all they can to get into the wedding banquet—but are shut out. The doorkeeper says, "I don't know you." This does not mean these people were never saved; it means they are not recognized or qualified to enjoy the wedding banquet.

This is why the coming of the bridegroom in the parable of the ten virgins must be applied two ways: the coming of the Lord Jesus through the Holy Spirit in great power and the physical coming of Jesus. But, I repeat, the parable omits the details we might expect regarding Jesus's physical coming. It is as though the parable puts the physical coming of Jesus to one side and does not mention it again until the parable of the sheep and the goats later in Matthew 25.

The point Jesus wants to make in this part of our parable is to show the sadness of those who blew their inheritance away by not taking oil in their lamps. It was a horrible moment to be told: "I don't know you." This is a word from the gatekeeper. In ancient Middle Eastern weddings the gatekeeper knew all the names of the people in the area. But only the wise virgins were recognized.

The coming of the Bridegroom by the Spirit therefore shows how the bride of Christ will have made herself ready. It is when the church is revived in holiness, evangelism, and in signs and wonders. The "readiness" of the bride is what I wrote about in chapter 13, "The Awakened Church."

This, then, is when King Jesus defeats His enemies by His Word, as seen in Revelation 19:11–16, the passage quoted at the beginning of this chapter. The coming of the Spirit in power is described in these verses. King Jesus is seen as defeating all His enemies by the Word of God in verses 11–15. Jesus Himself in person is *still* seated at the right hand of God. He personally orchestrates the final move of the Holy Spirit from above. This is precisely what makes the bride "ready" for the wedding between herself and the Lamb (v. 7).

The actual marriage is described later in the Book of Revelation:

> I, John, saw the Holy City, the New Jerusalem, coming down out of heaven from God, prepared as a bride adorned for her husband.
> —REVELATION 21:2

You will recall that the bridegroom came while the foolish virgins were on their way to buy oil. This part of the parable simply shows that the foolish virgins were desperate to rectify their folly. As Esau tried to persuade his father, Isaac, to give him the patriarchal blessing, so the foolish virgins will go on bended knee to the wise for mercy. But it was too late. He could find no place for repentance, though he sought it diligently with tears (Heb. 12:17).

THE FOOLISH VIRGINS
AFTER THE MIDNIGHT CRY

Here is what will happen to the foolish virgins after the Midnight Cry. Having been awakened, those Christians who had not pursued their inheritance will do what they can to repent. They may try all sorts of spiritual exercises. They might try to get heavily involved in church work. They will go on bended knee to the wise virgins—Christians who are filled with the Holy Spirit—and beg them to pray for them. To lay hands on them. To do anything that might change God's mind. But as

I mentioned earlier, an oath had been sworn. There was nothing they could do.

While this is going on, the Holy Spirit begins to fall on the church in great power. Unprecedented power. The coming of the Bridegroom in the power of the Spirit gives the church unprecedented power in gospel preaching, evangelism—millions being converted—and in signs and wonders.

PARALLEL BETWEEN PALM SUNDAY AND THE MIDNIGHT CRY

We noted earlier that as John the Baptist preceded the first coming of Jesus, so will the Midnight Cry precede the second coming. A parallel is also to be seen between the event of Palm Sunday and the coming of King Jesus in the power of the Holy Spirit. On Palm Sunday Jesus came into Jerusalem riding on a donkey. The event was prophesied by Zechariah: "Your king is coming to you" (Zech. 9:9). But He ended up on a cross.

However, the coming move of the Holy Spirit is described in the Book of Revelation as King Jesus riding on a white horse and defeating His enemies by the Word of God. The Palm Sunday event was the occasion of Israel's King being offered to them. But they wouldn't have it. He was not the king they wanted. So they crucified Him. But the next event will see the King of kings manifesting His power through the Word. The two-edged sword that comes from His mouth will slay His enemies. This time Israel will openly acknowledge their King as being the same Jesus of Nazareth who came to them two thousand years ago. It will be part of the outcome of the bride making herself ready.

The armies of heaven, following Jesus on white horses, therefore point to those whose ministries in the very last days will result in countless conversions to Christ, including millions of Muslims and millions of Jews coming to Christ. Palm Sunday led to Israel's King being rejected; the next great move of God will result in Israel's King being joyfully accepted by Jews.

Although what follows overlaps somewhat with what I have already said above, here is what you can expect to happen before Jesus leaves His throne in heaven:

The church will be equipped to evangelize with an optimum level of an understanding of the Word and measure of the Holy Spirit. This will be largely the work of evangelists who were wise virgins, as we saw in a previous chapter.

Jesus will defeat the power of Islam's hold on millions of Muslims. For years there have been countless Muslims who have had visions of Jesus, convincing them (1) that He is truly the Son of God and (2) that He died on a cross. Muslims believe Jesus was only a "prophet." Furthermore, Allah would not allow a prophet to die on a cross; therefore they do not believe that Jesus actually died on the cross. They believe Allah delivered Jesus from dying and took Him straight to heaven. This robs Jesus of His glory and diverts people from seeing the power of His blood.

But Jesus will manifest His glory to millions of Muslims, not only showing them through dreams but also through evangelistic efforts of the church. I cannot be sure how this will transpire. I predict, however, that key Muslim leaders will have the courage to tell of their own dreams and will come out of hiding to confess what was revealed to them by the Holy Spirit. We are talking of millions, not merely thousands. This will also make Jews envious (Rom. 11:11). This is why I would have thought that the conversion of Muslims will precede the lifting of the blindness of Jews.

The blindness on Israel will be lifted. This is what Paul implicitly predicts in Romans 11. Whereas he does not say categorically that the blindness of Israel will be lifted—rather that He is "able" to do so (v. 23), the underlying thrust of Paul's language leads us to believe that the blindness *will* be lifted.

I think, however, there is a reason that Paul did not say explicitly in Romans 11 that the blindness will absolutely and inevitably be lifted; otherwise all of us might become complacent and not bother to evangelize Jews. I know of Christian leaders who believe we should not evangelize Jews, that they are inevitably going to come to the Lord in the end. Some even teach that Jews get a second chance. Wrong.

This is horribly wrong. It is dangerous, even, as it were, sending them to hell.

I recently wrote a letter to Prime Minister Benjamin Netanyahu. I lovingly cautioned him that the situation in Israel today will not get better until Jews turn to Jesus Christ. I promised him that if the Jews turned to the Lord, the God of Israel would start fighting for them as He did in ancient times. I'm sorry, but God is certainly not fighting for them at the moment. We do the Jews no favor to let them think that they don't need to worry about their security since they are God's chosen people. Jeremiah was accused of treason for prophesying that the Babylonians would destroy Jerusalem. Jeremiah was right.

These things said, I do believe that Israelis and Jews will turn to Jesus Christ in mass numbers in the end. It will be a part of Jesus making all His enemies His footstool. In any case, "all Israel will be saved" (Rom. 11:26). That means that the *elect* Jews—of which there will be millions—will turn to Christ and, if I have gotten this right, in a very short period of time. Paul made it clear that not all who are Jews—or Israelites—are God's children, but only those chosen (Rom. 9:6–15).

All non-Christian religions will turn to Jesus Christ in mass numbers. This means Hindus, Shintoists, Buddhists, Mormons, Jehovah's Witnesses, Taoists, and, as we said, Muslims, will bow to King Jesus as being *God in the flesh.*

Death will be destroyed. Jesus must reign "until He has put all enemies under His feet. The last enemy that will be destroyed is death" (1 Cor. 15:25–26). Here is how this will happen. While *still on His throne* Jesus will raise the dead as He raised Lazarus from the dead (John 11:43). He may even speak with a loud voice again! The dead will rise, and Jesus will then—not before—leave His throne at God's right hand. This is when the physical second coming of Jesus takes place, as we will see in the next chapter.

You might ask: Is not Satan himself an enemy of Jesus—and will Jesus defeat and punish Satan before He leaves His throne? I reply: Satan will be defeated in two stages: (1) by defeating all of Satan's *allies* Jesus will defeat Satan from the Father's right hand, and (2) Satan himself will be thrown into the lake of fire to be punished forever and ever (Rev. 20:10). Jesus could easily do either from His throne—by His mere Word.

This brings us to the next event as described in the parable of the ten virgins—the wedding banquet.

CHAPTER 15

THE BANQUET

Those who were ready went in with him to the wedding banquet.
—MATTHEW 25:10

*Let us be glad and rejoice and give Him glory, for the
marriage of the Lamb has come, and His wife has made
herself ready.... Then he said to me, "Write: Blessed are those
who are invited to the marriage supper of the Lamb."*
—REVELATION 19:7–9

*And I saw an angel standing in the sun, and he cried with
a loud voice to all the birds flying in the midst of heaven,
"Come and gather for the supper of the great God, to eat the
flesh of kings, the flesh of commanders, the flesh of strong
men, the flesh of horses and their riders, and the flesh of
all men, both free and slave, both small and great!"*
—REVELATION 19:17–18

W HAT COMES TO YOUR MIND WHEN YOU THINK OF A
banquet? A long table with beautiful white tablecloths,
crystal glasses, and the finest of silver ware with the choicest of foods—
filet mignon steaks, lobster, caviar, turkey, and smoked salmon?

Caution: the wedding banquet in Revelation is different from any
other banquet in history.

The menu is different.

Take, for example, the Lord's Supper. It is a spiritual meal; one does
not eat the bread or drink of the wine to get physically satisfied. It is
entirely spiritual and for our edification.

The marriage supper of the Lamb will be eaten not to feed our bodies but to thrill our souls with unspeakable joy and glory—all because we witness the glorious and final defeat of Jesus's enemies:

> Come and gather for the supper of the great God, to eat the flesh of kings, the flesh of commanders, the flesh of strong men, the flesh of horses and their riders, and the flesh of all men, both free and slave, both small and great!
> —REVELATION 19:17–18

Jesus had forecast the Lord's Supper when He said, "Truly, truly I say to you, unless you eat the flesh of the Son of Man and drink His blood, you have no life in you" (John 6:53). This was the ultimate "hard saying" of John 6. It was so offensive that many of Jesus's disciples turned back and no longer followed him (v. 66). He did not destigmatize His remarks by saying, "Please don't desert Me; I am only referring to what will be known as Holy Communion later on." No.

Likewise John does not explain what is meant by "eat the flesh of kings, the flesh of commanders, the flesh of strong men," etc. The meaning is this: as eating the flesh of Jesus meant spiritually feasting on Him who is the bread from heaven (John 6:41), so eating the flesh of these people meant feasting upon the victory of the Word of God, which had slain the enemies of Jesus. For out of Jesus's mouth came a "sharp sword" with which to strike down the nations. Jesus was seen as having a sharp two-edged sword coming out of His mouth (Rev. 1:16). It was therefore the Word of God that defeated all of Christ's enemies—the cults, the false teachings of the world, and those who had laughed and scorned the true gospel.

SATAN'S PARTY IS OVER—FOREVER

The marriage supper of the Lamb is the celebration that the bride of Christ has made herself ready. It will be the most delicious and satisfying feast in the history of humankind. That is, for believers. All others will weep, wail, and gnash their teeth. It is when the Christian faith is vindicated before the entire world.

But for the great intellects of this world—the Cambridge dons, the scientists of Harvard and Yale, the politicians, the liberals of theological

seminaries, the rich and famous who had ridiculed the gospel of Christ—
the great banquet means, "The party's over." A different kind of party
has begun.

That is what happened when King Belshazzar gave a great banquet for
a thousand of his nobles. They "drank wine and praised the gods of gold
and of silver, of bronze, of iron, of wood, and of stone" when suddenly
"fingers of a man's hand appeared and wrote opposite the lampstand on
the plaster of the wall." The king watched the hand as it wrote. His face
turned pale, and he was so frightened that his knees knocked together
and his legs gave way (Dan. 5:1–6).

The marriage supper of the Lamb will signify that "the party's over"
for those who've scorned the gospel and that a new party has begun—
the wedding banquet. We will be rejoicing in the greatest movement of
the Holy Spirit since the days of the early church.

How would you like to be right in the middle of the greatest move of
the Holy Spirit since Pentecost? That is precisely what the wise virgins
will be privileged to enjoy. They are the ones invited into the wedding
banquet. "Blessed are those who are invited to the marriage supper of
the Lamb" (Rev. 19:9). "Those who were ready went in with him to the
wedding banquet" (Matt. 25:10).

Note that they "went in *with him* to the wedding banquet." This
refers to the *person* of the Holy Spirit. The wedding banquet is Jesus's
phrase for the mighty move of God at the end times. It promises an
intimacy with the person of the Holy Spirit. It will be the Lord fighting
His enemies with His two-edged sword in the power of the Spirit. This
will demonstrate the highest level of the Holy Spirit in the history of the
church. Therefore, as this is the spiritual coming of the Lord, so will the
next and final move of God on the earth mean fellowship with the Holy
Spirit unlike anything the people of God have ever experienced.

The great supper of the Lord will not fill people's bellies but will fill
their hearts and minds with unimaginable satisfaction, contentment,
peace, and absence of petty jealousies that have so long divided the body
of Christ. It will be a case of men and women loving the glory of the
Lord more than the praise of one another.

At long last these scriptures that point to an "Omega Point" in history will be fulfilled:

> But truly as I live, all the earth will be filled with the glory of the LORD.
>
> —NUMBERS 14:21

> Be exalted, O God, above the heavens; may Your glory be above all the earth.
>
> —PSALM 57:5

> For the earth shall be full of the knowledge of the LORD as the waters cover the sea.
>
> —ISAIAH 11:9

> For the earth will be filled with the knowledge of the glory of the LORD, as the waters cover the seas.
>
> —HABAKKUK 2:14

Bible students and scholars have asked the question: When will these promises be fulfilled? There are two basic answers: either before or after Jesus returns. That said, if the knowledge of the glory of the Lord will cover the earth only after Jesus returns, there is nothing to look forward to but the second coming itself.

However, these verses will be fulfilled *before* the physical second coming of Jesus. All this will happen while Jesus is still at the Father's right hand. King Jesus will be orchestrating the greatest move of the Holy Spirit since Pentecost, resulting in the bride making herself ready. God has determined that the church, the bride of Christ, should be without spot or wrinkle.

Is it possible that the church could be holy and without blemish *before* the second coming? Yes, *relatively* speaking. The church will not be pure and spotless in an absolute sense before the second coming. For only the second coming of Jesus—which takes place simultaneously with our glorification—can cause the church to be without blemish, stain, or wrinkle in an absolute sense. Then, and only then, will we all be totally changed—when this mortal will put on immortality (1 Cor. 15:53). As we will see below, glorification is the ultimate state of grace of the justified

(Rom. 8:30). We shall be changed into Christ's likeness. "We shall be like Him, for we shall see Him as He is" (1 John 3:2). After Jesus personally comes—and only after this—we will be totally without sin.

The bride "making herself ready" takes place prior to the second coming of Jesus Himself. It will be like ancient Israel conquering Canaan. It will be like the Book of Acts all over again, except with greater power than ever.

But don't forget the suffering. Not all will be saved. Not all will be convinced. And yet it will be the bride making herself ready.

That is what is promised.

Those who are invited—namely, the wise virgins—will be right in the middle of the greatest move of the Spirit since Pentecost. It will be their inheritance—their reward—for persistent faith in pursuing the Word and the Spirit.

Those who are shut out—namely, the foolish virgins—will weep and gnash their teeth with sorrow for their lack of gratitude to the Lord for the gospel that saved them. Try to imagine what people like this will go through. Their sense of regret will be impossible to describe except to put it in terms of weeping and gnashing their teeth.

A word to all Christians: you don't need to be a foolish virgin.

THE FOOL

At the end of his tragic life King Saul stated, "I have played the fool" (1 Sam. 26:21, KJV). The MEV says "acted foolishly." King Saul became "yesterday's man" because he was not accountable to anybody and put himself above Scripture (1 Sam. 13:9–13). He did not merely "happen" to be a fool; he *chose* to be a fool.

So with the foolish virgins. Those who are called "foolish" made a choice to be foolish. "They...did not choose the fear of the LORD" (Prov. 1:29).

The designation "fool" in the Bible is never imputed to a person with a natural lack of intelligence, something that he or she cannot help. The fool in the Bible *chose* to be a fool. Partly what makes a fool a *fool* is that the person is, in fact, intelligent. Being a fool is an act of the will. The fool, or foolish, in the Bible describes a person who willfully but unnecessarily made imprudent choices. "As a dog returns to its vomit, so a fool returns to his folly" (Prov. 26:11). Whereas keeping God's commands "will keep you from the immoral woman" (Prov. 7:5), the fool lets the adulteress lead him astray, little knowing "it would cost him his life" (v. 23).

Perhaps the greatest malady of a fool is that he or she seldom—if ever—admits to being wrong.

I have wanted this book to serve as a wake-up call to those Christians who sadly come into the category of "foolish virgins" because of wrong choices. A word to such people: *you don't have to remain a foolish virgin.*

PART 3
JESUS PERSONALLY COMING TO JUDGE

CHAPTER 16

THE SAME JESUS

When He had spoken these things, while they looked, He was taken
up. And a cloud received Him from their sight. While they looked
intently toward heaven as He ascended, suddenly two men stood
by them in white garments. They said, "Men of Galilee, why stand
looking toward heaven? This same Jesus, who was taken up from you
to heaven, will come in like manner as you saw Him go into heaven."
—ACTS 1:9–11

He will appear a second time, not to bear sin but
to save those who eagerly wait for Him.
—HEBREWS 9:28

[Jesus Christ] whom the heavens must receive until
the time of restoring what God spoke through all
His holy prophets since the world began.
—ACTS 3:21

For He will reign until He has put all enemies under His
feet. The last enemy that will be destroyed is death.
—1 CORINTHIANS 15:25–26

A YOUNG MAN NOTICED A TRACT LYING ON THE PAVEMENT IN
Kensington High Street in London. He picked it up and read it.
It was my tract "What Is Christianity?" He prayed the prayer at the end
of the tract and was instantly converted. The following Sunday he made
his way to Westminster Chapel since there was a map of the chapel on
the back page of the tract. He introduced himself, and it was so thrilling
to discover how my tract was used in this man's life.

A few weeks later he was baptized. Sometime after that he came up to me to share a discovery he thought he had made from reading the Bible—that Jesus Christ is coming back one day. "Is this true?" he asked.

"It certainly is," I replied.

He looked so excited. "This is wonderful, isn't it?" he added joyfully.

"Yes. It is wonderful."

When one has grown up to believe in the second coming of Jesus, as I have, it is easy to take it for granted and forget the dazzling truth that Jesus Christ—born in Bethlehem, raised up in Nazareth, who died on a cross and was raised from the dead—is coming back again. As the angels said to the disciples, "This *same* Jesus" will return to the earth. We are therefore talking about the literal, physical, and personal return of the man Jesus.

Do you believe this? I'm afraid some sincere believers have almost given up on this truth. Perhaps they have lost heart, became discouraged, or were influenced by those who do not believe the Bible in the first place. Peter refers to "scoffers" who say, "Where is the promise of His coming?" (2 Pet. 3:3–4).

But let's be fair. Are *all* "scoffers" who wonder if Jesus is really and truly coming back again—or who do not believe the second coming will necessarily take place in our day? After all, Peter wrote that almost two thousand years ago. Furthermore, he merely said that there would be scoffers to speak like this; it does not mean that all who are discouraged are scoffers.

Surely one can understand those who say, "I've heard this teaching all my life. People have been saying this for two thousand years. Why should I believe this or believe He is coming soon?" I know of people even in the twentieth century who quit their jobs and refused to purchase health or life insurance, all because they became convinced that Jesus was coming in a week or two. Their miscalculation has led to other Christians no longer believing in the "soon" coming of the Lord Jesus.

But what about those words of Jesus right at the end of the Book of Revelation? "Surely I am coming soon," He said (Rev. 22:20). That was quoted by the apostle John in around AD 100, more than nineteen hundred years ago. This is not easy to explain. The phrase "last days" has always been cloaked in some mystery. John said that he knew it was the "last hour" because of the coming of the Antichrist and that "many anti-christs" have come (1 John 2:18). That was in ca. AD 90. The writer of Hebrews also speaks of "these last days," meaning that Jesus Christ's first coming fulfilled the predictions of the forefathers and prophets of the past (Heb. 1:2). According to the writer of Hebrews, then, the "last days" began once Jesus arrived on the scene.

What is going on here? We might begin by noting that with God a thousand years is like a day and a day like a thousand years (2 Pet. 3:8). I know also what it is like to have a vision and think it will be fulfilled a week later. I have been waiting sixty years for some of them to come to pass!

What then does the Lord mean by "soon"? Is it "soon" from His point of view? It is certainly not soon from our point of view. "Soon" there-fore must be understood from God's point of view since a thousand years with God is like a day. That said, Jesus would have known what all of us would regard as soon! We would have thought it meant days or months or—at the most—a very few years. So why would Jesus say, "I am coming soon," knowing as He did that we would take this to mean He would have come within a few years after He said that?

BREAKING THE BETRAYAL BARRIER

I answer: this comes under the category of *breaking the betrayal barrier.* This means not only to overcome what appear to be impossible conditions but also persisting in faith when we feel that God has utterly betrayed us. Who we thought was a close and reliable friend suddenly seemed like an enemy. I therefore bring in a caution: that God only *seems* to betray us. The greatest saints in biblical history had this in common: they felt betrayed by God but broke the betrayal barrier. Martin Luther even said that you must know God as an enemy before you can know Him as a friend.

Abraham, for example, was promised Canaan as an inheritance, but Stephen pointed out that God gave him "no inheritance in it, nor a foot-hold" (Acts 7:5). In his commentary on this verse John Calvin observed that Abraham must have felt deceived.[1] Not only that, consider those described in Hebrews 11 who did great exploits by faith, "*but they did not* receive the promise" (Heb. 11:39, emphasis added)! Think about that for a moment. These great people of faith—Enoch, Noah, Abraham, Isaac, Jacob, Joseph, Moses, Samuel, David, and others—*did not receive* what God Himself promised them! We may ask: Why ever didn't they give up? Why did they persist in faith? Were they out of their minds? Were they extraordinarily simple? Were they naïve? Obscurantists?

No. They all broke the betrayal barrier, a feat that not all accomplish. It is from my pastoral experience that I suggest that perhaps one in ten professing Christians keep relying on God and persevering in faith after they feel betrayed by Him. If there is a sudden death of a child, infidelity by a spouse, betrayal by a close friend, financial reverse, losing a job, or a major leader who falls morally, many people abandon their faith. But perhaps one out of ten keep on believing and relying on the faithfulness of God when feeling betrayed by Him. And yet *why* these believers press on makes no sense to many. Why ever do such people *not* turn their backs on God? Why did they keep on believing?

I think the answer can only be because God had been so real to them at some stage. To put it another way, Jesus had been so real and so precious to them that it kept them from giving up. They had seen God work so powerfully in their lives that they were not going to let an extreme trial make them quit. Take the ancient martyr Polycarp (*d.* AD 155), for example. When he was about to be burned at the stake and asked to renounce Jesus Christ and praise Caesar, Polycarp replied, "Eighty and six years have I served Him, and He never did me any injury: how then can I blaspheme my King and my Saviour?"[2]

So with those listed in Hebrews 11. They knew it would be worth it to press on. As a consequence of persisting in faith against seemingly insurmountable odds, each of them turned their world upside down. "The world was not worthy of them" (Heb. 11:38). They did what they did by persistent faith.

In a word: each of them broke the betrayal barrier.

Aeronautical science broke the sound barrier in the twentieth century when planes flew faster than the speed of sound. It was a major accomplishment. But a far, far greater achievement is to break the betrayal barrier. It is when you hit a wall and feel deserted, let down—betrayed—by the same God who had been so real to you. All those who are described in Hebrews 11 had this in common—they broke the betrayal barrier. That is what sovereign vessels do.

This too is my reply to the old argument that the Bible contradicts itself, as when the Word of God states that Jesus is coming soon even though He has not come back after two thousand years of waiting. God's ways are higher than our ways. "For as the heavens are higher than the earth, so are My ways higher than your ways, and My thoughts than your thoughts" (Isa. 55:9). It is well put by Rick Warren: "Any apparent contradiction in Scripture is [due to] my limited capacity."[3]

This is why I still believe in the second coming. What is more, I believe He is coming soon—even by *my* understanding of soon! But could I be wrong? Yes.

I will say it again, I am so glad that Jesus did not come before July 13, 1935—or I would not have been born! I am so glad that He did not come before April 5, 1942, or I would not have been saved!

What about you? Do you not have reason to be thankful that He has *not* come back to the earth so far?

And yet because it has been so long since we were given these promises, some theologians have given up on a literal second coming and have come up with alternative explanations.

The truth is, more is taught about the second coming by New Testament writers *after* Jesus ascended to heaven than by Him before He died on the cross. This may surprise you, but it is not as easy as you might think to amass a number of Jesus's own sayings regarding the second coming. They are there, yes, but they are relatively few. Why? I believe the answer is, Jesus knew how much His disciples could take in. "I have yet many things to tell you, but you cannot bear them now" (John 16:12). Among the things Jesus did not state *often* and *explicitly* was His second coming. They are mostly to be found in Matthew 24, Mark 13, and Luke 21. Like other things Jesus said that could not be grasped until after Pentecost, so too His teaching that not only would He be raised from the dead and taken to heaven but also He would return to the earth a second time. That would have been too much to bear. That said, once the Holy Spirit had come, His disciples could recall

His teachings on Mount Olivet as in these three previously mentioned chapters.

I put alternative explanations to a literal second coming below. Although these are false views, some of them have a measure of merit.

ALTERNATIVE VIEWS PERTAINING TO A LITERAL SECOND COMING

Personal conversion

Some say that the second coming of Jesus is merely one's personal conversion. Some speak of conversion as the Lord "coming into my heart." As I heard one preacher put it, "Jesus came the first time to die on a cross; He came the second time to enter my heart." It is true that the Lord comes into our hearts when we are saved. Paul used the phrase "Christ in you, the hope of glory" (Col. 1:27).

> What a wonderful change in my life has been wrought
> Since Jesus came into my heart.
> I have light in my soul which so long I had sought
> Since Jesus came into my heart...
> Floods of joy o'er my soul like the sea billows roll,
> Since Jesus came into my heart.[4]
>
> —R. H. McDaniel

How true! How wonderful! Conversion is indeed Jesus coming into our hearts. But conversion is not the second coming of Christ. The angels said to the disciples, "This same Jesus, who was taken up from you to heaven, will come *in like manner as you saw Him go* into heaven" (Acts 1:11, emphasis added). Jesus was "taken up" before their very eyes. "And a cloud received Him from their sight" (v. 9). Since He is to come back in the same way they saw Him go into heaven, coming visibly with the clouds, this rules out conversion as a valid explanation for the second coming.

Acts 1:11 and 1 Corinthians 15:26 ("The last enemy that will be destroyed is death") are arguably the best defense against all the erroneous views that follow.

The coming of the Holy Spirit

Some have opined that Jesus's return after His ascension to heaven was fulfilled when the Spirit of God came down on the disciples at Pentecost. For example, consider these words: "For the Son of Man shall come with His angels in the glory of His Father, and then He will repay every man according to his works. Truly I say to you, there are some standing here who shall not taste death before they see the Son of Man coming in His kingdom" (Matt. 16:27–28). The reference to Jesus coming in His Father's glory with His angels sounds an awful lot like other verses that clearly infer the second coming. But when Jesus added, "There are some standing here who shall not taste death before they see the Son of Man coming in His kingdom," we are compelled to apply this to Pentecost.

Probably some of them who heard these words were around at the time of the coming of the Spirit at Pentecost. And yet did they "see" the Son of man on the Day of Pentecost? Perhaps in a sense they did, and perhaps Jesus did come in the person of the Spirit along with angels at Pentecost.

In any case, this passage would lend itself to the weightiness of the claim that Pentecost rather than the second coming was taught by Jesus. This is further suggested by Mark's treatment of the same account: "Truly I say to you, there are some standing here who will not taste death before they see the kingdom of God come with power" (Mark 9:1). Almost certainly this is a reference to the Holy Spirit coming down at Pentecost.

One can therefore see the reason some combine what are thought to be references to the second coming to the coming of the Spirit. Many have applied Jesus's words, "I will come again and receive you to Myself, that where I am, you may be also" (John 14:3), to the second coming. But some think it is a reference to the coming of the Spirit.

After all, Paul did say that we are seated with Christ "in the heavenly places" (Eph. 2:6). By this Paul meant that all Christians—now—are seated with Christ in the heavenlies. This means we are lifted up by the Holy Spirit to have intimate fellowship with Him. Moreover, Jesus would be as real to us by the Spirit as He previously had been to the disciples before He ascended. He said to them, "In a little while you will not see Me; and then after a little while you will see Me" (John 16:17). This explains how real Jesus was to the 120 on whom the Spirit fell at Pentecost.

These things said, apart from what we have seen in Acts 1:11, Peter preached that "the heavens must receive [Jesus] *until* the time of restoring what God spoke through all His holy prophets" (Acts 3:21, emphasis added). In other words, these words of Peter came sometime after Pentecost, clearly showing that the early church did not believe that the coming of the Spirit at Pentecost was Jesus's physical return. Furthermore, the last enemy to be destroyed is death. This is to say nothing about more of Paul's teaching of the second coming—to be examined below—a doctrine he claimed to have received from Jesus Himself.

The destruction of Jerusalem ca. AD 68

This too is a weighty point. For one of the most recondite pursuits in biblical interpretation is understanding Matthew 24, Mark 13, and Luke 21. It is not easy to figure out which of Jesus's statements refers to His second coming and which refers to the destruction of the temple in Jerusalem. Some interpreters would say that these passages *only* refer to Caesar's armies destroying the temple. Some also think these passages refer only to the second coming. But both interpretations are surely meant, and yet it is not so easy to differentiate between the verses that refer to the second coming and those referring to the destruction of Jerusalem.

Jesus frequently used an intentional ambiguity in His parables, and He does so in these chapters, commonly called the Olivet Discourse. The statements in Matthew 24, Mark 13, and Luke 21 were precipitated by (1) Jesus's observation regarding the temple and (2) the disciples' questions. First, Jesus said of the temple: "Truly I say to you, not one stone shall be left here upon another that shall not be thrown down" (Matt. 24:2). "When you see Jerusalem surrounded by armies, then you know that its desolation has drawn near" (Luke 21:20). This was Jesus's prophecy foretelling the destruction of Jerusalem, which, in fact, came about some forty years later (ca. AD 68). As Jesus was sitting on the

Mount of Olives, the disciples came to Him privately. They asked, "Tell us, when will these things be, and what will be the sign of Your coming and of the end of the age?" (Matt. 24:3). Whereas Jesus initially referred to one thing—the destruction of the temple—the disciples' question referred to two if not three things: (1) "When will these things happen" (i.e., the destruction of the temple), (2) "What will be the sign of Your coming" and (3) "the end of the age?"

The issue turns on what is meant by "Your coming." It could possibly mean the Lord Jesus showing up in judgment on Jerusalem in AD 68, hence His "coming." But other verses in the Olivet Discourse only refer to His second coming. How do we know some verses refer to the second coming? There are several reasons, listed below, not the least of which is the reference to the coming of the Son of man in "the clouds of heaven with power and great glory" (Matt. 24:30). This is eschatological language—cohering with Jesus's being taken up in a cloud and returning to the earth the same way, as stated in Acts 1:9–11. This therefore implies far more than the destruction of the temple. For example, leaving out other verses that could almost certainly be used, here are six references that point only to Jesus's second coming and not to the destruction of Jerusalem:

- The gospel of the kingdom will be preached "throughout the world as a testimony to all nations" and then would the end come (Matt. 24:14).

- As lightning that comes from the west is visible in the east, "so will be the coming of the Son of Man" (Matt. 24:27).

- The Son of man will "appear in heaven, and then all the tribes of the earth will mourn" (Matt. 24:30; see also Rev. 1:7).

- The Lord will send His angels with "a great sound of a trumpet, and they shall gather His elect from the four winds, from one end of the heavens to the other" (Matt. 24:31; see also 1 Cor. 15:52; 1 Thess. 4:16).

- No one knows the day or the hour this will come (Matt. 24:36). Whereas it could be said that no one knew the day or the hour when Caesar would march into Jerusalem, the following verses—Matthew 24:37–41—make little sense if you apply them to the event of AD 68. They show therefore that verse 36 refers to the second coming. Note: it is a predestined date that only the Father knows.

- The last enemy to be destroyed is death (1 Cor. 15:26). As long as people are dying, you may be sure Jesus has not come yet.

The possible third question of the disciples regarding "end of the age" also appears as being eschatological. Some have argued that the end of the age was only the culmination of the generation following Jesus's ascension, but it makes far more sense for the end of the age to mean the last day (i.e., the final end). Jesus said that people will defend their good works to Him in "that day," which clearly is eschatological. This indicates the final judgment following His second coming. He said that "many will say to *me* on that day, 'Lord, Lord, did we not prophesy in your name. . . .' Then I will tell them plainly, 'I never knew you'" (Matt. 7:22–23, NIV, emphasis added). The end of the age would therefore not refer to AD 68 but the eschatological end—this still being future.

In a word: the Olivet Discourse includes both the destruction of the temple in Jerusalem in AD 68 and the second coming. This is why I said that the argument that the second coming took place in AD 68 is weighty. We know, however, that the destruction of Jerusalem was not the second coming. But here are two more reasons: (1) the previously quoted words of Acts 1:11 and (2) the fact that the Book of Revelation, written some thirty years after the destruction of the temple, refers again and again to the future coming of Jesus.

The spreading of Christianity

The exponential growth of the church of God throughout the world, say some, is Jesus's coming back a second time. However, Jesus said that the gospel must be preached to all nations as something that *preceded* the second coming but not the same thing as the second coming. That said, the amazing growth of the Christian faith was truly a vindication of the teachings of Jesus Christ and the apostles. But some want to say that the very diffusion of Christianity all over the world is Jesus coming a second time. We go back to Acts 1:9–11, which stipulates that the second coming is His return to the earth in the same physical body He had when He ascended from the Mount of Olives.

The intervention of Jesus in judgment

"I will come to you," said Jesus to the angel of the church of Ephesus. It was a promise of judgment if the church did not repent. "I will come to you quickly and remove your candlestick from its place, unless you repent" (Rev. 2:5). We can quickly dismiss this as being Jesus's second coming if only because so much of the Book of Revelation points to the future coming of Jesus and that He would come with "clouds." Indeed, He will be seen by "every eye...even those who pierced Him. And all the tribes of the earth will mourn because of Him" (Rev. 1:7).

And yet this account does show that Jesus can execute judgment from the Father's right hand—without leaving His throne and coming personally to the earth. This would also suggest that the death of Herod, carried out by the angel because Herod did not give praise to God but welcomed people calling him a "god," was orchestrated by the Lord Jesus Himself. We would have to say the same thing about the sudden deaths of Ananias and Sapphira for lying to the Holy Spirit (Acts 5:1–10); it was what the Lord Jesus did from His heavenly throne.

It is essential to remember this: Jesus does not have to leave His throne at the Father's right hand to carry out judgment! Or to defeat His enemies. Indeed, it is promised by David that the coming Messiah will not leave God's right hand until He makes all His enemies His footstool (Ps. 110:1). If Jesus can execute judgment from God's right hand, it is equally true that He is the architect of any revival to the church—from earliest days to the present.

No other Old Testament verse is quoted more often in the New Testament than Psalm 110:1, and it is most relevant for the parable of the ten virgins. Is the second coming referred to elsewhere in the Old

Testament? I'll explore the answer to this question in the next chapter. Before you read on, remember: the second coming, which we are examining in this part of the book, will not take place until Christ has made all His enemies His footstool.

CHAPTER 17

THE SECOND COMING IN THE OLD TESTAMENT

I will put enmity between you and the woman, and
between your offspring and her offspring; he will
bruise your head, and you will bruise his heel.
—GENESIS 3:15

The LORD said to my lord, "Sit at My right hand,
until I make your enemies your footstool."
—PSALM 110:1

THE TEACHING OF THE SECOND COMING OF JESUS IS NOT A NEW
Testament innovation. That God's Messiah was predestined to
come not once but *twice* was initially predicted in the Garden of Eden
and repeated in various places in the Old Testament.

I cannot recall hearing a sermon on the second coming of Jesus as I
grew up that was based on an Old Testament passage of Scripture. All
sermons I heard as a child and teenager came from the four Gospels, the
New Testament Epistles, and the Book of Revelation. I thought therefore I should say something in this book about the second coming as
forecast in the Old Testament.

Never forget that the early church did not have the twenty-seven
books of the New Testament as we have it but *only* the thirty-nine
books of the Old Testament. All references to Scripture in the New
Testament meant the Old Testament (2 Tim. 3:16; 2 Pet. 1:20–21).
When the Bereans "examined the Scriptures every day to see if what
Paul said was true" (Acts 17:11, NIV), this meant that they consulted
the Old Testament. Peter's sermon on the Day of Pentecost was based
entirely upon Old Testament passages (Acts 2:16–35). Paul's support for

the death and resurrection of Jesus was "according to the Scriptures" (1 Cor. 15:3–4)—meaning the Old Testament.

I have a prediction in this regard. It is something I have believed and preached for years. When the Midnight Cry comes about and the church is revived, there will be an astounding return and attachment by believers to the Old Testament. Instead of the Old Testament being vague and dark (as it seems to be to some), it will come alive and relevant to a wonderful degree. The early church saw things in the Old Testament that are not recorded in the New Testament. I predict that we will see what they saw! If you ask, How did Peter know that Psalm 16 referred to the resurrection of Jesus?, the answer is: by the revelation of the Holy Spirit. In the same way, there are many passages in the Old Testament that refer to Jesus. Some of these scriptures are mentioned in the New Testament; some are not. My point is this: we will one day soon see things for ourselves from reading the Old Testament—insights given to them that we had not remotely thought of. The early church saw them; what they saw is but the tip of the iceberg in what is found in our New Testament. This refers to the first coming of the Messiah and what He came to do—but also the second coming.

The first coming of the Messiah two thousand years ago took everyone by surprise. The last thing they dreamed of was that He would die on a cross. The long-awaited prophet of whom Moses spoke—"a prophet from the midst of you, of your brothers" (Deut. 18:15)—was crucified. The Jews refused to recognize Him as their promised Messiah. And yet Isaiah foresaw this hundreds of years in advance: "Who has believed our report? And to whom has the arm of the LORD been revealed?" (Isa. 53:1). Near the beginning of the fourth Gospel John noted: "He came to His own [the Jews], and His own people did not receive Him" (John 1:11). Why did they not recognize Him? Two reasons may be given. First, they assumed that the true Messiah would be a charismatic military and political leader who would overthrow Rome. They envisaged another David or Solomon. Those two kings represented the "glory days" of Israel. This kind of figure was the only type of Messiah they could imagine.

Second, Israel missed their Messiah because of their low spiritual state. They had wandered far from God. Had they been where they ought to have been spiritually, they would not have missed Him. But they were in a deeply backslidden state. For example, the idea of pursuing the honor of God—which they should have done—did not cross their minds. Knowing as He did that the Jews generally did not believe in Him, Jesus asked: "How *can* you believe, who receive glory from one another and do not seek the glory that comes from the only God?" (John 5:44, emphasis added). Jesus was virtually saying, "You are *unable* to believe in Me because you are not the slightest bit interested in the honor and glory of God. You only want praise from each other." In other words, had the Jews been right with God, their hearts would have responded to Jesus from the beginning. That then is the real reason the Jews not only did not recognize their Messiah but also demanded His death on a cross.

These things said, the notion of a second coming was even more remote from them. Even His most devoted followers would have struggled with the notion of Jesus coming a second time! It was one thing to reject Jesus as Messiah in the first place; it's quite another to take on board that Messiah did not come to overthrow Rome but to forgive sins. The kind of leader the Jews envisaged was not entirely off the mark; after all, the Son of God coming in power and justice was the sort of Messiah they wanted in the first place. The essence of the second coming was making His enemies His footstool. Indeed, Jesus would not leave His throne in heaven until He made His enemies His footstool!

But this was hard to take in. Even the disciples closest to Jesus struggled with this. They kept waiting for Him to explain *when* He would "restore the kingdom to Israel" (Acts 1:6). The meaning of the death and resurrection of Jesus passed by them entirely. They would not grasp this until ten days later at Pentecost. In the meantime, they were told clearly and specifically that this same Jesus would come back—in clouds like the way they saw Him ascend. It was a lot to take in.

Possibly the biggest thing to take in was that the second coming of Jesus was in the Father's mind since creation. The very fact that Jesus was the Lamb slain "before the creation of the world" (1 Pet. 1:20) proves that the second coming was in God's mind from the beginning. Do you think that Jesus decided to come back a second time because He failed in His mission by accepting death on a cross? No! The purpose of Jesus's first coming was to fulfill the Law by a sinless life and sacrificial death on the cross. It was God's predestined plan that Jesus would come first to "bear the sins of many" and then "appear a second time, not to bear sin but to save those who eagerly wait for Him" (Heb. 9:28).

We will look at some of the Old Testament references to the second coming.

GENESIS 3:15

The first promise of the second coming of Jesus is in Genesis 3:15. It was equally the promise of the first coming of the Messiah. "I will put enmity between you and the woman, and between your offspring and her offspring; he will bruise your head, and you will bruise his heel." These cryptic words followed the exposure of the sin of Adam and Eve. Here is the basic meaning of Genesis 3:15:

- First, the word was directed at the devil; God Himself addressed the serpent that had deceived Adam and Eve in the Garden of Eden.

- Second, there would be an eternal enmity between Satan and Jesus Christ.

- Third, Jesus would crush Satan's head. This crushing would be twofold; two events would be separated in time by at least two thousand years: (1) Jesus would defeat Satan at the cross, and (2) He would crush Satan's head a second time before leaving His throne, making all His enemies His footstool.

- Fourth, Satan would strike Jesus's heel. This took place when Jesus died on the cross. I would add that the crushing of the *head* means complete victory; the bruising of the *heel* was small by comparison.

There is a real sense in which Satan crucified Jesus. But it backfired on him. This is the meaning of the words: "None of the rulers of this age knew it [God's wisdom]. For had they known it, *they would not have crucified the Lord of glory*" (1 Cor. 2:8, emphasis added).

GENESIS 49:10

Jacob gave his patriarchal prophecy concerning his twelve sons. Judah, from whose loins Messiah would come generations later, gets the lion's share of this prophecy. But at least two things stand out. First, "Judah is a lion's cub; from the prey, my son, you have gone up. He crouches and lies down like a lion; and as a lion, who dares rouse him?" (Gen. 49:9). It is a fact that Jesus was born of the seed of David, who was of the tribe of Judah (Matt. 1:3–6). Indeed, "The Lion of the tribe of Judah, the Root of David, has triumphed. He is able to open the scroll and to loose its seven seals" (Rev. 5:5). Second, Jacob prophesied, "The scepter shall not depart from Judah, nor a lawgiver from between his feet, until Shiloh comes; and to him will be the obedience of the people" (Gen. 49:10). I refer specifically to the words "to him will be the obedience of the people." This refers to Psalm 110:1, to be cited again in a few paragraphs. It means that all of Jesus's enemies will become His footstool—a clear reference to the victory of Jesus over His enemies prior to the second coming.

JOB 19:25

This verse pretty much speaks for itself: "For I know that my Redeemer lives, and He will stand at last on the earth." This sounds like the second coming of Jesus to me! Where Job got this and how he came up with words like this is a mystery. It came right in the middle of his self-centered defensiveness against his "miserable comforters" as he called them (Job 16:2). Even if he did not grasp all he was saying, unworthy though he was, it could well be a case of a gracious God overruling the man who would be defended by God in the end. God sees the end from the beginning, and that is partly why He can be so gracious to us who are unworthy!

PSALM 110:1

This is arguably the strongest and most important messianic passage in the Old Testament: "The LORD said to my lord: 'Sit at My right hand until I make your enemies your footstool.'" Consider the way Jesus Himself used this psalm in Matthew 22. Jesus asked the Pharisees a question when they said that Messiah would be the son of David: "If David then calls Him 'Lord,' how is He his Son?" (v. 45) No one could answer Him. It was an affirmation that Messiah would be "Lord," that is, *God*. This psalm points to the ascension of Jesus—where Jesus was seated in heaven—and where He is right now: at God's right hand. The psalm also points to the priesthood of Christ, that the Messiah would be "a priest forever after the order of Melchizedek" (Ps. 110:4). The reference to the second coming, however, is when God affirms that Jesus will be at the Father's right hand "*until* I make your enemies your footstool." This means that when Jesus's enemies become His "footstool," He will return to the earth.

JUDE 14

This verse is obviously from the New Testament, but I insert it here because it refers to Enoch, the man who "walked with God, and then he was no more because God took him" (Gen. 5:24). The writer of Hebrews refers to him: "By faith Enoch was taken to heaven so that he would not see death. He was not found, because God took him away. For before he was taken, he had this commendation, that he pleased God" (Heb. 11:5). Jude quotes from apocryphal literature—not because we are to believe all else that is written in it, but obviously some of it was valid or Jude would not have quoted from it: "Enoch, the seventh generation from Adam, also prophesied of these men, saying, 'Look! The Lord is coming with ten thousand of His holy ones, to execute judgment on everyone, and to convict all who are godless of all their wicked deeds that they have committed, and of all the terrible words that godless sinners have spoken against Him'" (Jude 14–15). The amazing thing is this: Enoch, who walked with God and who pleased God, was at some stage lifted into the heavenly realms and saw the second coming of Jesus thousands of years away! Note too its connection with the final judgment.

1 SAMUEL 2:10

This word is from the prophetic exultation by Hannah, the mother of Samuel: "For by strength shall no man prevail. The adversaries of the LORD will be broken to pieces; He will thunder against them out of heaven. The LORD will judge the ends of the earth" (1 Sam. 2:9–10).

I am not saying that Hannah saw the second coming of Jesus as clearly as we do now, but she was without doubt given a glimpse of the sovereignty of God. What she said coheres with later words, that the glory of the Lord will cover the earth as the waters cover the sea (Hab. 2:14).

PSALM 2:8–9

This messianic psalm prophesies the inheritance of Jesus Christ. This would be fulfilled while Jesus is at the right hand of God anticipating His return to the earth: "Ask of Me, and I will give you the nations for your inheritance, and the ends of the earth for your possession. You will break them with a scepter of iron; you will dash them in pieces like potter's vessel" (Ps. 2:8–9).

PSALM 96:13

This too is a messianic psalm that anticipates the second coming and final judgment of Christ: "Let the heavens rejoice, and let the earth be glad; let the sea roar, and all that fills it; let the field be joyful, and all that is in it; then all the trees of the forests shall rejoice before the LORD, for He comes, for He comes to judge the earth. He shall judge the world with righteousness and the peoples with His faithfulness" (Ps. 96:11–13).

ISAIAH 2:4

If you ask a Jew today, "Why do you not believe that Jesus is Israel's Messiah?," the frequent answer is: "Because we still have wars." They base the opinion largely on verses like this one.

And yet, as I said above, what many in Israel saw as being the accomplishment of Jesus's first coming into the world is precisely what He will do with reference to His second coming: "He shall judge among the nations and shall rebuke many peoples; and they shall beat their swords into plowshares, and their spears into pruning hooks; nation shall not lift up sword against nation, nor shall they learn war any more" (Isa. 2:4).

ISAIAH 9:6–7

This glorious passage embraces the birth of Christ, the deity and office of Christ, plus His second coming in one full sweep: "For unto us a child is born, unto us a son is given, and the government shall be upon his shoulder. And his name shall be called Wonderful Counselor, Mighty God, Eternal Father, Prince of Peace. Of the increase of his government and peace there shall be no end, upon the throne of David and over his kingdom, to order it and establish it with justice and righteousness, from now until forever. The zeal of the LORD of Hosts will perform this" (Isa. 9:6–7).

ISAIAH 11:9

I insert this verse here because it is eschatological. It demonstrates my thesis that the Lord will make His enemies His footstool prior to the second coming: "For the earth shall be full of the knowledge of the LORD as the waters cover the sea" (Isa. 11:9).

ISAIAH 66:15–16

Isaiah foresaw the second coming of Jesus together with His judgment over all peoples: "For the LORD shall come with fire and with His chariots like a whirlwind, to render His anger with fury and His rebuke with flames of fire. For by fire and by His sword on all flesh, the LORD shall execute judgment; and the slain of the LORD shall be many" (Isa. 66:15–16).

DANIEL 7:13

There are several passages in the Book of Daniel to which one might refer that demonstrate the second coming of Jesus. Among these is the following passage that shows this without question: "I saw in the night visions, and there was one like a Son of Man coming with the clouds of heaven. He came to the Ancient of Days and was presented before Him. There was given to Him dominion, and glory, and a kingdom, that all peoples, nations, and languages should serve Him. His dominion is an everlasting dominion, which shall not pass away, and His kingdom that which shall not be destroyed" (Dan. 7:13–14).

HOSEA 13:14

A brief passage leaps out at us from the prophet Hosea. It is undoubtedly what gave rise to Paul's words in 1 Corinthians 15:25, to be seen in the next chapter. "I will ransom them from the power of Sheol [the grave]. I will redeem them from Death. O Death, where are your plagues? O Sheol, where is your sting?" (Hosea 13:14).

ZECHARIAH 14:4

This is a difficult verse and not easy to discern precisely how it will be fulfilled. But because of its being set in the context of the Day of the Lord (Zech. 14:1), I believe it refers to the second coming of Jesus. Not only that—which is so interesting, it suggests that the prophecy of the two angels is fulfilled to the degree that Jesus would not only return with clouds but even return to the same Mount of Olives from which He ascended (Acts 1:9–11). "On that day His feet will stand on the Mount of Olives, which is to the east of Jerusalem. And from east to west the Mount of Olives will be split in two halves by a very great valley so that one half moves to the north and the other to the south" (Zech. 14:4).

MALACHI 3:1

Like my use of Isaiah 11:9 above, I insert this verse not because it refers to the directly to the second coming but rather to the Midnight Cry before the second coming. Not only that; it also refers to John the Baptist. You may recall that I see the awakening before the second coming as a John the Baptist type of ministry: "I will send My messenger, and he will prepare the way before Me. And the Lord, whom you seek, will suddenly come to His temple, even the messenger of the covenant, in whom you delight. He is coming, says the LORD of Hosts" (Mal. 3:1).

The next great and move of God will come suddenly—on a day we least expect it.

CHAPTER 18

THE END OF DEATH AND THE FINAL RESURRECTION

For this we say to you by the word of the Lord, that we who are alive and remain until the coming of the Lord will not precede those who are asleep. For the Lord Himself will descend from heaven with a shout, with the voice of the archangel, and with the trumpet call of God. And the dead in Christ will rise first. Then we who are alive and remain shall be caught up together with them in the clouds to meet the Lord in the air. And so we shall be forever with the Lord.
—1 THESSALONIANS 4:15–17

Then comes the end when He will deliver up the kingdom to God the Father, when He puts an end to all rule and all authority and power. For He will reign until He has put all enemies under His feet. The last enemy that will be destroyed is death.... Listen, I tell you a mystery: We shall not all sleep, but we shall all be changed. In a moment, in the twinkling of an eye, at the last trumpet, for the trumpet will sound, the dead will be raised incorruptible, and we shall be changed. For this corruptible will put on incorruption, and this mortal will put on immortality. When this corruptible will have put on incorruption, and this mortal will have put on immortality, then the saying that is written shall come to pass: "Death is swallowed up in victory."
—1 CORINTHIANS 15:24–26, 51–54

HOW WOULD YOU LIKE TO RECEIVE YOUR THEOLOGY PERSONALLY and directly from the Lord Jesus Christ? This would be an unthinkable privilege. But this is the case with the apostle Paul. Admittedly some people—so unwisely—are quick to say, "The Lord told me," when it comes to biblical insight or prophetic utterances. But in the case of the apostle Paul, he really did get his soteriology and eschatology directly from Jesus. This happened shortly after his conversion. He said, "I did not immediately confer with flesh and blood, nor did I go up to Jerusalem to those who were apostles before me. But I went into Arabia, and returned again to Damascus" (Gal. 1:16–17). Then after three years he went to Jerusalem, where he met Peter and James (vv. 18–19).

There was therefore an era—which may have lasted up to fourteen years (Gal. 2:1)—during which Paul was given infallible knowledge of the pure gospel. Thus he did not receive his understanding from any man but "by a revelation of Jesus Christ" (Gal. 1:12). Imagine this: being tutored or spoon-fed by Jesus Himself.

This fact should help refute the notion of some who say "Jesus, yes; Paul, no" when it comes to their understanding of Christianity. What we get from Paul is from Jesus except when, at times, he admits he is offering his own opinion (e.g., in 1 Corinthians 7:12).

The "word of the Lord" expressions in Paul's writings refer specifically to his being directly taught by Jesus. For example, concerning the Lord's Supper he said, "I have received of the Lord that which I delivered to you," and then proceeded to give instructions that the church generally has followed ever since (1 Cor. 11:23–26). He also made this claim when it came to his doctrine of the second coming. What he taught them was "by the word of the Lord" (1 Thess. 4:15). Therefore keep in mind we are getting Paul's understanding of the second coming as if from Jesus Himself. We may wish that Paul told us more than he did when it comes to eschatology!

The Epistle of James is probably the earliest of the New Testament documents, likely being written between AD 44 and 48. James was the Lord's brother—technically, half brother. He was one of the weightiest leaders in the early church, having enormous prestige and respect by all. But we have no evidence that he was taught any more than what the eleven disciples knew. He had one reference to the second coming, found in James 5:8: "You also be patient. Establish your hearts, for the coming of the Lord is drawing near" (ESV: "at hand"). There is little doubt that the earliest Christians expected the second coming in their day—literally at any moment.

In fact, the widespread expectancy of the Lord's coming was so intense that it caused a crisis in some churches. This happened with the church in Thessalonica. Both of the letters to the church of Thessalonica address this issue. People panicked when some Christians *died*. They had somehow assumed they would all be alive when Jesus came. They feared that those who died must not be true believers—or they would still be alive. This is what caused Paul to bring in the second coming in his letters to the Thessalonians. They are Paul's earliest letters, written around AD 52.

Church history can be understood as a graph on a chart; there were low-water marks and high-water marks. The high-water marks would refer to times of refreshing, revival, a return to Scriptures, high church attendance, and excitement in the church. Low-water marks refer to an absence of excitement, disinterest generally in the things of God—and low church attendance. But when we come to those high-water marks— when the church is revived—there is almost always also a keen interest in the second coming of Jesus and expectancy that He is coming soon!

My old denomination (Church of the Nazarene) was born in revival. The early years were characterized by frequent preaching of the second coming of Jesus. Not only that; there was a widespread assumption that *Jesus is coming soon*. In my old church in Ashland, Kentucky, we had "revivals" three times a year—in the autumn, the winter, and the spring—all of them lasting at least twelve days. Those days are gone. Most revivals—if churches have them—are now held on weekends or for one day. But in those days of the two-week revival—and summer camp meetings that would last a week—there would always be at least one sermon on the second coming of Jesus and that His coming was at hand. When I was a teenager, I was deeply moved by a sermon based on Matthew 24:44: "Therefore be ye also ready: for in such an hour as ye think not the Son of man cometh" (KJV). I wept like a baby and remember telling the man who preached it, "This is the greatest service of my whole life." Years later, when I became pastor of my first church— in Palmer, Tennessee, in 1955—there was a lady who would frequently show up to sing the song "Wait a Little Longer, Please Jesus."

Such was the expectancy of the nearness of Jesus's coming that people were afraid He would come any second and that their loved ones would be lost. But such expectancy is gone. The Elim Pentecostal Church in the UK was born in revival. One of their major tenets was not just the second coming but the "soon coming" of Jesus. But genuine expectancy that Jesus is coming soon nowadays has sadly pretty much disappeared.

How many songs are written today about the second coming? There have been some good songs in our time and a lot of shallow ones—but very, very few about Jesus's coming again. The Midnight Cry will change this overnight.

Paul introduced his teaching of the second coming with these words: "But I would not have you ignorant, brothers, concerning those who are asleep, that you may not grieve as others who have no hope" (1 Thess. 4:13). The expression "asleep" was a euphemism for death. Jesus used this when referring to Lazarus's death: "Our friend Lazarus has fallen asleep. But I am going that I may awaken him from sleep" (John 11:11). His disciples did not comprehend that Jesus meant Lazarus was dead and that He would raise him from the dead. They took Jesus to mean that natural sleeping would be good for Lazarus, that he would get better. Then Jesus said to them, "Lazarus is dead" (v. 14). Paul therefore uses the same expression for those who were saved but who died; they were merely "asleep" (1 Thess. 4:13).

The major point Paul wants to establish is that those Christians who died—that is, "those who sleep in Jesus" (v. 14), whom he also refers to as the "dead in Christ" (v. 16)—will be the first to be raised when Jesus returns. Therefore not only do they have "hope"; God will bring those who have fallen asleep "in Jesus" when He returns. This also shows their souls—or spirits—are with Jesus now. It means their bodies will be raised from the dead simultaneously with His return. Their spirits will be reunited with their newly resurrected bodies. Paul continues: "*By the word of the Lord* [what Paul received by revelation], that we who are alive and remain until the coming of the Lord will not precede those who are asleep" (v. 15, emphasis added). Indeed, the dead in Christ are raised first, then those who are alive will be "caught up together with them" (v. 17).

The second coming of Jesus will openly prove that He destroyed death from the Father's right hand. He will not leave His throne until He has put all enemies under His feet (Ps. 110:1; Acts 3:21; 1 Cor. 15:25–26). The last enemy to be destroyed is death. The proof that death has been destroyed is that He raises them from the dead from His throne. As He raised Lazarus from the dead by His voice (John 11:43), so will He speak to the dead from His throne—and raise *all* the dead. Some have observed, perhaps humorously, that had Jesus not called out Lazarus's name in Bethany, all the dead throughout the world would have risen from their graves then! In any case, Jesus will raise the dead by His voice from His place at God's right hand. He will then leave His throne *with those* who have died in Christ to meet Christians in the air who are alive at this time.

There will there be two sorts of Christians directly involved in Christ's second coming: (1) those who are alive when He comes, and (2) those who have died. Those who have died are raised first. How much time elapses between the resurrection of the dead in Christ and those who are "caught up"? The answer is given in 1 Corinthians 15:52: "in the twinkling of an eye"—as quick as the batting of an eyelash. This means that those alive and those who are resurrected are "with the Lord" virtually at the same time.

And yet Paul teaches that *all* people will be resurrected on the day of the second coming. This would include saved and lost. Jesus taught there would be a resurrection of both the righteous and wicked. "Do not marvel at this," said Jesus. "For the hour is coming in which all who are in the graves will hear His voice and come out—those who have done good to the resurrection of life, and those who have done evil to the resurrection of judgment" (John 5:28–29). Daniel taught this hundreds of years before: "Many of those who sleep in the dust of the earth shall awake, some to everlasting life, but others to shame and everlasting contempt" (Dan. 12:2). This was Paul's position: "There will be a resurrection of the dead, both of the just and the unjust" (Acts 24:15). The problem for us is, Paul never tells us what the resurrected body of the wicked will be like. He only tells us that "we shall all be changed." This will come in that "twinkling of an eye" moment when the trumpet will sound and the dead will be raised imperishable (1 Cor. 15:51–54). By "dead" being imperishable he may have meant "dead in Christ," but for some reason he does not stipulate this. We are not told what the body of the unsaved will be like. In any case, this event will come when Jesus returns.

We all would like to be alive when Jesus comes again. I certainly would. I used to think I would be alive. Not that it was "revealed" to me; it is a natural wish. It *was* "revealed" to Simeon that he would not die until he had seen the "Lord's Christ." Simeon had got that right (Luke 2:25–32). I know of several who feel it was revealed to them that they would not die but be living when Jesus comes again. All these are dead. It is natural to want to escape dying. In any case, it is thrilling to know that one day we will be reunited with our loved ones. My mother has been with Jesus since 1953; my dad has been there since 2002. Martyn Lloyd-Jones has been with the Lord since 1981.

Therefore Paul's initial teaching of the second coming referred to the crisis of sincere Christians fearing that things had gone badly wrong since fellow believers had died. Not to worry, says Paul; they are with Jesus now, but when Jesus comes a second time, we will all be with the Lord—forever. Furthermore, we should "comfort one another with these words" (1 Thess. 4:18). The second coming is a "blessed hope"—a glorious appearing—when Jesus leaves His seat at the right hand of God and is joined by all His people (Titus 2:13–14).

However, another crisis emerged among the Thessalonians. There were those who taught that Jesus had already come! Some self-appointed prophets were claiming this. There were rumors that Paul taught this, and many were upset. So Paul wrote:

> Now, brothers, concerning the coming of our Lord Jesus Christ, and concerning our gathering together unto Him, we ask you not to let your mind be quickly shaken or be troubled, neither in spirit nor by word, nor by letter coming as though from us, as if the day of Christ is already here. Do not let anyone deceive you in any way. For that Day will not come unless a falling away comes first, and the man of sin is revealed, the son of destruction, who opposes and exalts himself above all that is called God or is worshipped, so that he sits as God in the temple of God, showing himself as God.
>
> —2 Thessalonians 2:1–4

This opens a different subject. We are now told that two things must take place before the Lord comes: (1) the rebellion and (2) the man of lawlessness comes. And yet Paul reminds them that he had taught this when he was with them in Thessalonica (v. 5).

Keep in mind that Paul received this from the Lord Jesus. This is not Paul expressing a private opinion. It is therefore to be taken most seriously. The rebellion, or great falling away, would probably refer to apostate Christianity.

But when did this emerge? Some think at the beginning of the second century when Christianity degenerated into moralism instead of salvation by grace. Some might say the rebellion came in the Middle Ages, known as the "dark ages," when Roman Catholicism prevailed until the time of the Protestant Reformation. That said, it is one of the most difficult areas of eschatology.

One of the most perplexing things is Paul's comment to them regarding the man of lawlessness, or man of sin: "*You know* what restrains him that he might be revealed in his time" (2 Thess. 2:6, emphasis added). Apparently the Thessalonians knew something we don't know, unless it was the basic teaching of the sovereignty of God to which Paul refers. He continues: "For the mystery of lawlessness is already at work. Only he who now restrains it will do so until he is out of the way" (v. 7, ESV).

God the Holy Spirit is the One who "now restrains it." This is the intervention of a sovereign God who restrains the mystery of lawlessness. Paul refers to two things: the *mystery* of lawlessness and the *man* of lawlessness. "The *mystery* of lawlessness is already at work. Only he who now restrains it will do so until *he* is taken out of the way." I conclude: the mystery of lawlessness is an "it"; the One who holds it back is God Himself. God will continue to hold this power of lawlessness back until "he"—the man of lawlessness—is taken away.

But who is he? That is the question! He is the embodiment of the spirit of lawlessness. He is commonly known as the "antichrist"; twentieth-century speculations included Stalin, Mussolini, Hitler, John F. Kennedy, the pope, and others. These speculations will continue. Some would opine that Muhammad is the man of lawlessness, that Islam is the mystery of lawlessness, or sin. One thing is certain: he will be overthrown and destroyed by the Lord Jesus—"with the breath of His mouth" and by "the brightness of His presence" (2 Thess. 2:8).

Until undoubted light is further provided for us, I personally think we have come as close as we can to an assured understanding of this extremely difficult aspect of eschatology.

CHAPTER 19

THE MANNER OF
JESUS'S SECOND COMING

Look! He is coming with clouds, and every eye will see
Him, even those who pierced Him. And all the tribes of
the earth will mourn because of Him. Even so, Amen.
—**REVELATION 1:7**

But the day of the Lord will come like a thief in the night.
—**2 PETER 3:10**

THE PHRASE "DAY OF THE LORD" GOES BACK TO THE OLD
Testament prophets (e.g., Isa. 27:1; Joel 3:12–14; Zeph. 1:14–18). It
signified a time when—at long last—God would roll up His sleeves and
step into the world with authority, power, *and* undoubted *just* judgment.
Whatever else is signified, it would be a scary time. It would be a day
of days. It was so much a part of many Israelites' way of thinking that
Jesus only needed to refer to "that day." "Many will say to Me on that
day, 'Lord, Lord, have we not prophesied in Your name?'" (Matt. 7:22).
The people present probably knew what He was talking about. It referred
to the final judgment when Christ Himself sits on the throne.

The Hebrew word *yom*—day—does not always mean a twenty-four-
hour day as we know it. It could refer to an era. That is what the Day
of the Lord will be like. Jesus will no doubt appear on a certain *day*, but
that day will almost certainly be a part of an extended period of time
that could go on for a while.

The culmination of this period known as the Day of the Lord will be
the final judgment. It will be the day when every knee bows and every
tongue confesses that Jesus Christ is Lord. It will be the time all secrets
are laid bare. It will reveal who is saved and who is lost, who will have

a reward at the judgment seat of Christ and who will be saved by fire. It will be the day when God clears His name and reveals the reason for evil in this world. The Day of the Lord, then, is an era. And yet the second coming will take place on a specific day.

What will the second coming look like? What will it be like? What are we to expect? In short, a grand spectacle of unprecedented awe will be on display before every eye in the whole world. A sight greater than any Fourth of July celebration, more exhilarating than any laser beam demonstration, more uplifting than what people felt on the day Churchill greeted thousands at the announcement of victory over Germany, more moving than any royal wedding in England—except for one thing: the lost will be sobbing their hearts out and not able to be enthralled by the sight. They will "wail" because of Jesus (Rev. 1:7, ESV). This wailing and grief will be heard and manifested by all the peoples of the earth.

Only the lost, then, will be among those watching and wailing before the Lord of glory. This is because only the lost will have been left behind. The saved will have been "caught up" with the sainted dead who were resurrected less than a second before. Jesus said, "Two will be in the field; one will be taken, and the other left. Two women will be grinding at the mill; one will be taken, and the other left" (Matt. 24:40–41). Those who are "taken" are those who are caught up; those who are left behind are the unsaved. Those who are caught up will be experiencing a greater joy and ecstasy than can be imagined.

There will be some readers who may ask: Is this the rapture? Yes. But it is not a secret rapture. It will be out in the open. What follows will be the judgment seat of Christ, not years of great tribulation as taught by some. As for a time of tribulation, we will go through this *before* the second coming—we will not be raptured out of it. Great tribulation has already begun in some parts of the world and will continue with horrible suffering during the time of the great awakening that precedes the second coming.

What about those who are lost and have been in their graves? Will they be resurrected? Yes. They will be resurrected to face their condemnation, as Jesus put it (John 5:29, NIV). They will be raised to face the terrible sight of the glorious King Jesus—and be made to stand before Him at the final judgment.

Here are other phenomena that will be connected with Jesus's second coming.

JESUS WILL COME WITH "CLOUDS"

Clouds are associated with the second coming. "Then the sign of the Son of Man will appear in heaven, and then all the tribes of the earth will mourn, and they will see the Son of Man coming on the clouds of heaven with power and great glory" (Matt. 24:30). "Hereafter you will see the Son of Man seated at the right hand of Power and coming in the clouds of heaven" (Matt. 26:64). "Then they will see the Son of Man coming in a cloud with power and great glory" (Luke 21:27). "Then we who are alive and remain shall be caught up together with them in the clouds to meet the Lord in the air" (1 Thess. 4:17). "Look! He is coming with clouds, and every eye will see Him, even those who pierced Him. And all the tribes of the earth will mourn because of Him" (Rev. 1:7).

What is the reason for the clouds? I offer two explanations. First, they are literal clouds that we all see daily in the sky. This demonstrates the *literalness* of the second coming, that Jesus will come bodily and visibly in clouds. This takes me back to a moment when I was a child, perhaps aged ten. I was on a roof of a house being built. My earliest pastor, Gene Phillips, was on this roof for some reason. He pointed to a large group of huge, fluffy, white cumulus clouds in the sky and said, "I think these are the kind of clouds Jesus will come back in." His words shook me rigid. I carefully climbed down from the roof—fearful I would fall—and found a secret place to pray for forgiveness of my sins. Not that I was not saved when I saw those clouds, but given my theology at the time, I had no assurance I was ready to meet the Lord. It was that experience of seeing those clouds that has stayed with me over the years and is partly the reason I have picked up on this aspect of the Lord's coming.

But there is a second possibility—and very likely, that the clouds will be the *shekinah* glory. This would mean they are not necessarily literal but rather the same type of cloud that entered the temple in Solomon's day (1 Kings 8:10–11; 2 Chron. 7:1). When Jesus was transfigured before the disciples, "a cloud came and overshadowed them" (Luke 9:34). If then this is what is meant by Jesus coming with clouds, it would probably mean that the cloud that hid Jesus from the disciples' eyes as He ascended was the *shekinah* rather than physical clouds.

HE WILL COME WITH THE SOUND OF A TRUMPET

Jesus will "send His angels with a great sound of a trumpet, and they shall gather His elect from the four winds, from one end of the heavens to the other" (Matt. 24:31). "For the Lord Himself will descend from heaven with a shout, with the voice of the archangel, and with the trumpet call of God. And the dead in Christ will rise first" (1 Thess. 4:16). "Listen, I tell you a mystery: We shall not all sleep, but we shall all be changed. In a moment, in the twinkling of an eye, at the last trumpet, for the trumpet will sound, the dead will be raised incorruptible, and we shall be changed" (1 Cor. 15:51–52).

The use of the trumpet, especially in a time of battle, goes back to the days of Moses and the children of Israel. "But when the assembly is to be gathered together, you will blow, but you will not sound an alarm. The sons of Aaron, the priests, will blow the trumpets, and they will be to you as an ordinance forever throughout your generations. And if you go to war in your land against the enemy that oppresses you, then you will blow an alarm with the trumpets, and you will be remembered before the LORD your God, and you will be saved from your enemies. Also in the day of your gladness, and at your appointed days, and in the beginnings of your months, you shall blow the trumpets over your burnt offerings, and over the sacrifices of your peace offerings that they may be a memorial for you before your God. I am the LORD your God" (Num. 10:7–10).

Paul said rather curiously that the second coming will happen with the sound of the "last" trumpet. What does this mean? I am not sure unless it means "it's over." The final judgment is at hand. The vindication of Jesus has come. You've probably heard the expression, "It ain't over 'til it's over." But the appearance of the second coming means it's *over*. There will be no further need of trumpet blasts. This is why it is called the "last day" (John 12:48). And yet some Bible students may want to apply the meaning "last" trumpet to the seventh trumpet as unveiled in the Book of Revelation (Rev. 11:15–19).

THE SECOND COMING WILL BE VISIBLE

It will be out in the open for everyone to see. "For as the lightning comes from the east and flashes to the west, so will be the coming of the Son of Man" (Matt. 24:27). Indeed, "Then the sign of the Son of Man will appear in heaven, and then all the tribes of the earth will mourn, and they will see the Son of Man coming on the clouds of heaven with power and great glory" (v. 30). Perhaps the whole of the Book of Revelation can be summed up at the beginning of it: "Look! He is coming with clouds, and *every eye will see Him*, even those who pierced Him. And all the tribes of the earth will mourn because of Him" (Rev. 1:7, emphasis added).

When one goes to a concert, watches a parade, or attends a public event, there is always the question of a good view. You pay more for a good seat at a play or concert. If you watch a parade, you hope that the person in front of you will not be too tall.

If you are not saved and are concerned about not getting a good glimpse of Jesus on this day of days, not to worry. You will have a front-row seat. Not only that; you won't be conscious of those around you. They will be sobbing and wailing too. They won't be conscious of you. You won't be conscious of them. It will be as if you are the only one there. For, after all, you have only one soul. You will realize you have lost it all. Jesus asked, "For what does it profit a man if he gains the whole world and loses his own soul?" (Mark 8:36).

IT WILL COME LIKE
A THIEF IN THE NIGHT

"But the day of the Lord will come like a thief in the night" (2 Pet. 3:10). This means Jesus will come when you least expect Him. He Himself said, "Therefore keep watch, because you do not know on what day your

Lord will come. But understand this: If the owner of the house had known at what time of night the thief was coming, he would have kept watch and would not have let his house be broken into. So you also must be ready, because the Son of Man will come at an hour when you do not expect him" (Matt. 24:42–44, NIV).

This part of the Olivet Discourse closes with Jesus's exhortation to be ready at all times (vv. 45–51). In the middle of the Book of Revelation are these words of Jesus: "Look, I am coming as a thief. Blessed is he who watches and keeps his garments on, lest he walk naked and his shame be exposed" (Rev. 16:15).

JESUS WILL BE ACCOMPANIED BY ANGELS

"Whoever therefore is ashamed of Me and of My words in this adulterous and sinful generation, of him will the Son of Man also be ashamed when He comes in the glory of His Father with the holy angels" (Mark 8:38). Have you ever seen an angel? You will see them then—probably billions of them.

JESUS'S COMING WILL BE ACCOMPANIED BY FIRE

Paul said that Jesus will be revealed from heaven "in flaming fire taking vengeance on those who do not know God and do not obey the gospel of our Lord Jesus Christ" (2 Thess. 1:8). When the Day of the Lord comes, "the heavens will pass away with a loud noise, and the elements will be destroyed with intense heat. The earth also and the works that are in it will be burned up" (2 Pet. 3:10). For that day will bring about "the day of God, in which the heavens will be destroyed by fire and the elements will be consumed by intense heat" (v. 12).

I cannot imagine what this will be like, nor can I say for sure what the role of the fire is. Is it the fire of hell? Is it the fire of which Paul speaks in 1 Corinthians 3:15, referring to Christians who will be saved by fire because their works were burnt up? Does the fire come initially with the trumpet blast? Or with the clouds? Or could it be that Paul and Peter are referring to the *era* I mentioned at the beginning of this chapter. Not all will happen at once. It could be, then, that the fire that accompanies the second coming will be a part of the era and not merely on the actual day Jesus comes.

This much is certain: the day of days is coming. It will be a dreadful, terrible day—except for those who confess Jesus Christ as Lord now. Now is the accepted time. Now is the day of salvation.

CHAPTER 20

THE PURPOSE OF
THE SECOND COMING

For He has appointed a day on which He will judge the world
in righteousness by a Man whom He has appointed.
—ACTS 17:31

But we know that when He appears, we shall be
like Him, for we shall see Him as He is.
—1 JOHN 3:2

HAVE YOU EVER WONDERED WHY GOD DID NOT CHOOSE TO accomplish *complete* redemption through the first coming of Jesus? By complete I mean three things: (1) the total eradication of our sinful nature, (2) the absolute healing of the body, and (3) the end of physical dying. This would have meant becoming just like Jesus as soon as we were saved by faith. In other words, glorification at conversion. After all, we are predestined to be conformed to the likeness of Jesus, "that He might be the firstborn among many brothers" (Rom. 8:29). Why did not God accomplish this *in one shot* when we were converted—and not spread it out over two thousand years or more? Glorification means sinless perfection, total healing of the body, and being transformed to be like Jesus.

Paul outlined what may be called the golden chain of redemption: "And those whom He predestined, He also called; and those whom He called, He also justified; and those whom He justified, He also glorified" (v. 30). God grants three of these four components of our salvation at our conversion as a result of Jesus's first coming: being predestined, called, and justified. But not glorified. Why did He not do all four—including glorification—through Jesus's first coming?

He could have. It would have been easy for God to do that. For that matter, God could have stopped Adam and Eve from sinning in the first place—or created them unable to sin. But that is not the way God chose to do things. Instead God created humankind "able to sin," as St. Augustine put it. Augustine actually put forward four stages of humankind's redemptive process: (1) able to sin—the way God created Adam and Eve, (2) unable not to sin—the condition of all humankind after the Fall in the Garden of Eden, (3) able not to sin—what we are like after being converted, and (4) not able to sin—as we will be when we are in heaven.[1] Yes, God could have chosen to do it differently had He wanted to. He is sovereign, omnipotent, and free to do what He chooses to do. But He had a different idea. Why? You tell me.

In any case, God has done what He chose to do. This meant that our salvation is to be perfected only by our glorification at Jesus's second coming. For when we see the glorified Jesus face to face, "we shall be like Him, for we shall see Him as He is" (1 John 3:2). Seeing His face will do it. He is therefore coming a second time not to bear sin but to bring salvation—that is, complete and perfected salvation—to those who are waiting for Him (Heb. 9:28). Paul referred to complete salvation when he said, "For now our salvation is nearer than when we believed" (Rom. 13:11). You might like to know that Augustine was converted through the preaching of Ambrose on Romans 13:11–14.

I now offer five reasons for the second coming of Jesus. These are not listed in order of importance, nor am I suggesting which of these comes first.

REASONS FOR THE SECOND COMING

1. Our glorification

This takes place when our bodies are *resurrected if we died* before the second coming, or *transformed if we are alive* at the time of the second coming, as we saw in a previous chapter. In this section I only want to show that our glorification is one of the reasons for the second coming of Jesus. All who ever lived will be raised on the day Jesus comes back. For some reason Paul does *not* explain what the resurrected body of the *unsaved* will be like. But glorification it certainly won't be; it is a term used only for those who have been justified by faith. "Those he justified, he also glorified" (Rom. 8:30, NIV). Glorification therefore takes place at Jesus's second coming. This event is future for all of us—including the countless millions who lived during the period between the fall of Adam and the coming of Jesus two thousand years ago—and all who died since. All of us need to be glorified in order to enter heaven. Why? Because we are sinners. We are imperfect in mind and body. Like it or not, "The heart is more deceitful than all things and desperately wicked" (Jer. 17:9). That is, beyond cure in this life. But glorification will cure it!

We were rendered unable not to sin by the Fall. This is the condition we inherited from birth. We were all born sinners. "I was brought forth in iniquity, and in sin my mother conceived me" (Ps. 51:5). We came from our mother's womb speaking lies (Ps. 58:3, NIV). This is why we must be taught to do right. We did not need to be taught to do wrong. It is called original sin. No human being who ever lived was exempt from this. Part of this inheritance, moreover, is not only the tendency to sin but also the inherent need to prove ourselves. It is a fruit of self-righteousness. We are born that way. It is the reason we all naturally feel that we can make it to heaven by good works. Every other religion under the sun—no exception—is based upon man's attempt to earn our way by good works. Isn't that interesting? But only the Christian religion offers salvation by pure grace alone—not of works (Eph. 2:8–9). This is one of the reasons why Christianity is so repugnant to the natural man or woman.

Once we are justified by faith in the blood of Jesus, we are given a power to be able not to sin, as Augustine put it. But that does not mean that we can attain to sinless perfection. If only.

I was brought up to believe in two works of grace: being "saved and sanctified." Sanctification was defined as "entire sanctification," based on 1 Thessalonians 5:23: "I pray to God that your whole spirit, soul, and body be preserved blameless unto the coming of our Lord Jesus Christ." This was taught to me as being attainable by a second work of grace. My introduction to this teaching was when at the age of six I burnt my tongue on my mother's cooked oatmeal. I was angry with her for making it so hot! She said to me, "You won't be like that when you get sanctified." I caught that sanctification meant the eradication of the carnal nature, the result being that one no longer lost his temper.

The truth is, said Paul, "the flesh lusts against the Spirit, and the Spirit against the flesh. These are in opposition to one another, so that you may not do the things that you please" (Gal. 5:17). We are "able not to sin," said Augustine, but this did not mean that the sinful nature has been taken away. It is always there—day and night, reminding us that we are not perfect. Perfection comes only from being glorified.

This is to say nothing about the imperfection of our *bodies*. God can heal today, and sometimes does. But there are sincere Christians who pray for healing—and receive prayer for healing—but are not healed for some reason. Not to worry, dear friends. Total, absolute, irrevocable healing will take place when Jesus comes again!

For the believer, glorification is achieved by the resurrection of our bodies. The resurrection of the body applies to all of the dead—saved and lost. Only the dead in Christ will be "glorified." Strangely, nothing is said about the nature of the resurrected bodies of the unsaved. All of the saved will be given transformed bodies. This takes place at the second coming of Jesus. "We shall all be changed," said Paul. "In a moment, in the twinkling of an eye, at the last trumpet, for the trumpet will sound, the dead will be raised incorruptible, and we shall be changed. For this corruptible will put on incorruption, and this mortal will put on immortality" (1 Cor. 15:51–53). This means not only the total eradication of our sinful nature but also the lifting of the curse that brought about death to the human race. The result will be no more sinning, no more sickness, no more disease, no more pain, no more crying, and no more death (Rev. 21:4).

What is more, we won't need faith to achieve this. *God will do it the moment we see Jesus!* It won't be via a process. It won't be because someone who has the gift of healing prays for us. It will not require the anointing of oil. No faith will be required; the sight of Jesus will do it—in a flash.

2. The vindication of Jesus

On the day that "every eye will see Him" (Rev. 1:7)—this being every person who ever lived at any time. These same people will now get on their knees and vindicate the Lord Jesus Christ. Not because they have been given new hearts but because they will be forced to admit who Jesus is. God has taken an oath—and has sworn by Himself—that all will bow to His Son. "As I live, says the Lord, every knee shall bow to Me, and every tongue shall confess to God" (Rom. 14:11).

The second coming will be a vindication of the *person* of Jesus and who He is. The Father exalted Jesus "and gave Him the name which is above every name, that at the name of Jesus every knee should bow, of those in heaven and on earth and under the earth, and every tongue should confess that Jesus Christ is Lord, to the glory of God the Father" (Phil. 2:9–11). The name that is above every name is *Yahweh*—the name of God. It will be God the Father's way of vindicating His Son as being "very God of very God," as Athanasius put it.[2]

It will be a vindication of all Jesus taught. He said, "He who rejects Me, and does not receive My words, has that which judges him. The word I have spoken will judge him on the last day" (John 12:48). The exultation of Jesus will be a vindication of His teaching about:

- Himself, about being the only way to the Father (John 14:6)

- The Holy Spirit (John 14–16)

- Seeking the honor that comes from God alone (John 5:44)

- The need to be born again (John 3:3)

- Believing on Him to receive eternal life (John 3:16)

- The need for the Father to draw people to Him (John 6:44)

- The flesh being of no profit (John 6:63)

- Being the eternal Word who existed not only before Abraham (John 8:58) but from the beginning (John 1:1)

- Perishing and eternal punishment (John 3:16; Matt. 25:41)

The second coming will be a vindication of all that Jesus accomplished on the cross. He claimed that He would fulfill the Law (Matt. 5:17, KJV). This meant living perfectly in thought, word, and deed—which He did (Heb. 4:15). Just before He died on the cross, He uttered the words, "It is finished" (John 19:30). This meant He completed the task set before Him and that He truly fulfilled the Law on our behalf.

It will be a vindication of His resurrection from the dead. When He was raised from the dead, He did not knock on Pilate's door Easter morning to say, "Surprise." He preserved the teaching that we believe in the literalness of the resurrection by *faith*. You and I are saved because we *believe* the word that Jesus died and rose again, not because we *saw* the risen Lord with our physical eyes.

The mockers at the cross said, "Let the Christ, the King of Israel, descend now from the cross, that we may see and believe" (Mark 15:32). Had Jesus come down from the cross, they would have *seen*. But their seeing would not be *faith* because faith—to be faith—is believing without seeing (Heb. 11:1). However, on that day of days every knee will bow and every tongue confess that Jesus is Lord because they all *see*. But it will be too late for them to believe so that their belief is truly *faith*.

Note one other thing: Paul mentioned "in heaven and on earth and under the earth" (Phil. 2:10); this was a reference to the demonic world. This means that Satan and all his fallen angels will openly confess before all men the truth about the Son of God!

The difference between the Christian and the non-Christian can be summed up this way: the Christian vindicates Jesus now; all the rest will vindicate Jesus on that day of days.

3. The total defeat of Satan

The devil has been around a long time. He has been the number-one adversary of God from before the fall of Adam and Eve. And yet God created him. God created all things. "For by [Jesus Christ] all things were created that are in heaven and that are in the earth, visible and invisible, whether they are thrones, or dominions, or principalities, or powers. All things were created by Him and for Him" (Col. 1:16).

But God did not create Satan as the evil creature he became. You may ask: Why did God create Satan able to do evil? I reply: I don't know. If you ask where the evil came from that Satan turned to, I don't know.

The problem of evil is the oldest issue in the universe and is utterly unsolvable until God chooses to unveil the reason for it—as we will see further below. All we know is that the evil serpent was in the Garden of Eden to tempt Adam and Eve in the beginning. Satan succeeded with them, and nothing was the same again.

My father used to say to me, "The devil is crafty, second only to God in wisdom and power." True. But do not forget that he is *second*. John reminds all Christians that the Holy Spirit "who is in you is greater than he who is in the world" (1 John 4:4). Satan can do nothing without God's permission. We learn this from the Book of Job; Satan has to have God's permission to do what he does (Job 1).

And yet Satan is the explanation for all the evil that is in the world. He is called the "ruler of this world" (John 12:31) and "the prince of the power of the air, the spirit who now works in the sons of disobedience" (Eph. 2:2). Satan is at war with God the Father, God the Son, God the Holy Spirit, and all those who know the Lord. Satan is at enmity with the good that is in the world. He is unthinkably evil and wicked. He has no heart for those who are suffering, no compassion for any human being—saved or lost. He exists with an icy hatred toward all of God's creation, especially those who are saved by the blood of Christ. He exists to abort any good work that comes from hearing the Word. As soon as people hear God's Word, the devil gets involved to take away the Word that is sown (Luke 8:12). He works day and night to gain entrance into our minds, taunting, tempting, and terrifying when he can.

Do not forget this: Satan has been given power to do evil anywhere in the world, whether by sending horrible weather—tsunamis, hurricanes, tornados; causing famine; exploiting those who suffer with poverty or illness; putting people in our paths who will tempt us or bring us down; robbing the people of God from having joy; interfering in our lives to divert us from noble plans; playing into our weaknesses to get us to grieve the Holy Spirit; making it hard to pray and read God's Word but making it easy to enjoy fleshly pleasures; taking advantage of the newest Christian to discourage them; testing the most mature saint where they are most vulnerable; knowing our strengths and therefore tempting us to pride; or knowing our weaknesses and ruthlessly tantalizing us to give up.

The devil is the explanation for all the hate, evil, hurting, and wickedness in the world. He holds the power of death (Heb. 2:14). He is the cause of pain, blindness, deafness, and all other physical and mental handicaps. He is the cause of people born with defective hearts or dysfunctional bodily organs. He is behind people wanting to abort their unborn; he loves abortion. He is the architect of family disunity, pornography, adultery, and prostitution.

He hates the Bible and will do all he possibly can to turn people from believing it—or reading it. He hates the blood of Jesus and will do all in his power to keep people from pleading the merit of Jesus's blood in their lives. He hates it when we pray; as William Cowper put it, "And Satan trembles, when he sees the weakest saint upon his knees."[3] Satan hates people going to church but loves it when the church ceases to worship God in Spirit and truth.

But his doom is coming—and he knows it. The demons shouted at Jesus, "What have we to do with You, Jesus, Son of God? Have You come here to torment us before the time?" (Matt. 8:29). Indeed, "he knows that his time is short" (Rev. 12:12). He therefore exists in perpetual, unimaginable fear. That is why he is an expert in causing us to fear; he wants to bring us down to his level. He is working overtime to do all the damage he possibly can before the second coming of Jesus.

But on that day of days Satan will be exposed before the entire world—and judged. His punishment will be everlasting torment in hell. He is the reason for hell—it was created for him (Matt. 25:41). He will be "cast into the lake of fire and brimstone," and he will be "tormented day and night forever and ever" (Rev. 20:10). The second coming will therefore bring about the total and irrevocable defeat and eternal punishment of Satan.

4. The vindication of God

This will be the day on which God clears His name. The secular atheist says, "God has a lot to answer for," that God is the cause of all the evil and suffering in the world, and even if God only "permits" evil,

He is to be blamed for permitting it. This is the rationale for unbelievers not to believe in God, not to believe that Jesus was raised from the dead, and not to believe the Bible.

Therefore these people say that God is the cause of all suffering (e.g., famine, war, bad weather, poverty, slavery, illness, prostitution, racism, injustice, the Hitlers of this world, and especially the harm that has come from religion). Whether Christian evangelicals or Islamic fundamentalists, they say, religious people have caused the most trouble in the world.

God has promised to clear His name one day. Habakkuk hoped to get the answer to the problem of suffering in his own day. But God said, in so many words, "Wait. I will reveal the reason I allow suffering on the last day."

Habakkuk might have said (as many might do), "That's not good enough. I want to know *now* so I can make sense of You."

"Sorry, Habakkuk, the vision speaks of the end and will be delayed for a while but will prove to be absolutely true—and will not lie" (Hab. 2:3).

Somehow Habakkuk accepted this. For God said that the just—righteous—will live by His faithfulness. Habakkuk was elevated to Abraham's category. God counted Abraham (called Abram at the time) righteous for believing His promise concerning Abraham's seed (Gen. 15:6); Habakkuk was counted righteous for his willingness to wait until the last day to know the answer to the problem of evil.

Habakkuk 2:4—"The just shall live by his faith"—is quoted three times in the New Testament (Rom. 1:17; Gal. 3:11; Heb. 10:38). How do we know that Habakkuk became willing not to get the answer to the problem of evil but to wait for the last day? The answer is that he said in the end (please remember that it was an agrarian society): "Though the fig tree does not blossom, nor fruit be on the vines; though the yield of the olive fails, and the fields produce no food; though the flocks are cut off from the fold, and there be no herd in the stalls—yet I will rejoice in the LORD; I will exult in the God of my salvation" (Hab. 3:17–18).

Habakkuk made a decision to vindicate God *now*. So should all Christians vindicate Him now by *faith*—even though we too do not have the answer to the problem of evil.

I can tell you now—categorically: the problem of evil is absolutely unsolvable. There is *no way* that the greatest mind—whether scientist, philosopher, or theologian—can explain the origin or reason for evil. The nearest you get is this: that we might have *faith*. God has blinded all our minds from seeing the reason for evil in order that we might have faith—which, as I said, is believing without seeing. Once God unveils the reason for evil and suffering—*and He will*—no faith will be needed. It will be seen even more clearly then that God has done us an incalculable favor not to unveil the reason He allows suffering. It is so we can believe without seeing—which is the only way God has decreed to be accepted and worshipped by people.

As to any other reason for suffering? God will tell us one day. I don't know how He will do it. One of two ways I would have thought: either by lifting off the blindness from us or explaining the reason in a way we could not have accepted or grasped. And when He does this, every mouth will be stopped. We will be stunned, or as my British friends would say, "gobsmacked." Our mouths will be hanging wide open. All will see then, but it will be too late for the unbelieving to believe.

God will clear His name when Jesus comes again.

5. The final judgment

Whether you call it "the judgment seat of Christ" (Rom. 14:10; 2 Cor. 5:10) or "a great white throne" (Rev. 20:11), the writer of Hebrews says, "As it is appointed for men to die once, but after this comes the judgment, so Christ was offered once to bear the sins of many, and He will appear a second time, not to bear sin but to save those who eagerly wait for Him" (Heb. 9:27–28). The writer immediately mentions the second coming, showing the inseparable connection between it and the final judgment. Paul does this also: "I charge you therefore before God and the Lord Jesus Christ, who will judge the living and the dead at His appearing and His kingdom" (2 Tim. 4:1).

Note this, that we do not stand before the judgment seat of Christ at the moment we die; the final judgment comes later. As we saw in chapter 18, our bodies will have been raised from the dead when we stand before the judgment seat of Christ. The final judgment immediately follows the second coming. In a word: all are raised from the dead at the precise time of second coming, and after that will come the judgment seat of Christ.

That said, judgment in some sense must be assumed before the second coming since God decides where we go when we die. Only the saved go to be with the Lord when they die; the lost do not. "The Lord knows those who are His" (2 Tim. 2:19). There is no judgment throne before which we stand the moment we die. We are instead immediately rewarded with great joy or punished with torment. This is why I say judgment in some sense has taken place: God judges who is in and who is out.

When we die, then, the Lord steps in and ensures that the saved go to be with Him. This means that God has already judged whether a person goes to heaven or hell. The parable of the rich man and Lazarus indicates that Lazarus died and immediately was carried by the angels to heaven where he was "comforted." The rich man went to hell (Gr. *hades*) where he was "in torment" (Luke 16:19–25). Paul believed that death means instantaneously going to be with Christ (Phil. 1:23).

John said he saw a great white throne "and *Him* who was seated on it" (Rev. 20:11, emphasis added). This is a reference to the Lord Jesus Christ. God has set a day when He will judge the world with justice by the man He has appointed—Jesus Christ (Acts 17:31). Note: it will be *justice* carried out at last. For example, God's judgment will far exceed the US Supreme Court in fairness and integrity. This is because the Lord Jesus Christ—who is "truth" (John 14:6)—will be doing the judging. Jesus said that many will say "to me" in that day, "Lord, Lord, did we not prophesy in your name?" (Matt. 7:22, NIV). It was Jesus saying right at the beginning of His ministry that one day He Himself will be the righteous judge.

Bear with me if I engage in a bit of speculation. For example, I have no idea how long it will take to carry out this judgment process. Though it will be a day of days, for all I know this "day" might take months or years. As we have seen, the Hebrew word *yom*, for example, may mean a twenty-four-hour day or an era. At any rate, all who stand before God will have been resurrected. We will have transformed bodies—like Jesus. I have no idea how we will be spending our time, but we will need no sleep and maybe no food. To what extent we eavesdrop on judgments that don't concern us, I can only guess. We will certainly be there for where we ourselves are concerned.

But remember: all people who ever lived will be there. John said, "And I saw the dead, small and great, standing before God" (Rev. 20:12). This means people of high profile as well as those people who were virtually unknown will be given full attention. But when it comes to the case of people like Adolf Hitler, we all are going to want to be there.

What then is the purpose of the final judgment? First, it will be to justify God's ways. This includes what we saw above regarding the vindication of God. Second, it will reveal the truth about all men and women who ever lived. It will be open before all. All secrets not covered by the blood of Christ will be out in the open. It will also show who is saved and why they are saved—namely, because they trusted the blood of Jesus—and who is lost and why they are lost. It will show who among the saved will be rewarded and who among the saved will have forfeited a reward. It will show why the lost are lost and what they have done to receive justly God's judgment on them. Unsolved crimes will be solved. Unjust judgments will be put right. Those who have suffered wrongly will be vindicated. Those who have been dishonest and cruel will be exposed and sentenced. The truth and motives of people like Adolf Hitler will be out in the open. The truth about nations and heads of state will be unveiled. The truth concerning doctrine that people squabble about will be unveiled. There will be no finger pointing then; every mouth will be stopped.

When Paul said that we must all appear before the judgment seat of Christ, he used the Greek word *bema*. You can go to ancient Corinth today and see where archeologists have found the original bema seat. It is a raised platform where people received rewards but also punishments. A winner of the Olympics, for example, would receive his garland at the bema seat. But it was also the place where the judge handed out sentences for a crime. Paul chose this word in writing to the Corinthians because they would know exactly what the bema seat was.

One aspect of the judgment seat of Christ, then, will be when Christians are openly rewarded for their obedience to God's Word.

Paul called it the "prize," and it was something very important to him: "Everyone who strives for the prize exercises self-control in all things. Now they do it to obtain a corruptible crown, but we an incorruptible one.... But I bring and keep my body under subjection, lest when preaching to others I myself should be disqualified" (1 Cor. 9:25, 27). The "prize" is not what gets you into heaven; it is what gives you a reward at the judgment seat of Christ.

Finally, the great white throne is where one is sentenced to eternal punishment. It is called being thrown into the "lake of fire" (Rev. 20:15). The good news is: anyone reading these lines need not go to hell. You can settle out of court, as it were—and do it now—by showing unfeigned sorrow for your sins, confessing them, and transferring your trust in good works to the blood of Jesus Christ.

CONCLUSION

THE FIRST PART OF THIS BOOK IS AN ELABORATION OF MY PROPHETIC analogy, namely, that the Pentecostal/Charismatic movement is not God's final move of the Spirit but nonetheless part of God's plan. Many Charismatics and Pentecostals have assumed that *they* were the final move of God. Wrong, in my opinion. As Abraham sincerely believed that Ishmael was the promised seed, so have many godly people thought that the Charismatic movement was the great revival to precede the second coming. But Isaac was the ultimate plan of God. As the promise concerning Isaac was a hundred times greater than the promise concerning Ishmael, so will the coming move of the Holy Spirit be infinitely greater than anything that has taken place on this planet since Pentecost. The purpose of this section is to encourage the reader that the best is yet to come—and that it is coming soon!

The second part of this book is my interpretation of the parable of the ten virgins. I have sought to show that the church today is in a deep sleep, that both the wise and foolish virgins are spiritually asleep. I believe that the wise and foolish virgins are not representative of saved and lost people but rather two categories of Christians: those who pursue their inheritance and those who do not. Please see chapter 5 for my view of what a foolish and a wise virgin are like. The main purpose of this book is to wake up the church and show Christians' responsibility to come into their inheritance by following the Word and the Spirit. I don't want any reader to be found to be a "foolish virgin" when the Midnight Cry comes. With that in mind, would you pray this prayer:

Lord Jesus, I thank You for the wake-up call that is given in this book. I don't want to be like the foolish virgins who did not pursue the Word and the Spirit. I pray that my life will be one that pursues the gifts and fruit of the Spirit equally—and earnestly. Please grant that I will be thrilled and not disquieted when the Midnight Cry comes. Amen.

The final section of this book has dealt with the fact of the personal, physical second coming of Jesus and the importance of being ready when He comes personally to judge all people. The most important question of all, therefore, pertains to whether you are ready for the second coming of Jesus Christ.

I close with two questions to you. First, do you know for sure that if you were to die today, you would go to heaven? I asked this question to a former prime minister of Great Britain. He replied, "Do you?" He thought it would be presumptuous to know for sure that one is going to heaven. This is because most people can't get their heads around the truth that salvation is by sheer grace and not works (Eph. 2:8–9). It is *not* presumptuous to know you will go to heaven. I said to the late Yasser Arafat, "The most important question you should deal with is not whether you or the Israelis get Jerusalem but where will *you* be one hundred years from now?"

My second question: If you were to stand before God (and you will) and He were to ask you (He might), "Why should I let you into My heaven?," what would you say? I must tell you, there is only one basic answer. And if the answer that comes to you is *not* trusting in the death of Jesus Christ on the cross, I must lovingly say to you that I would not want to be in your shoes for anything in the world. But that can be sorted out right now. Would you now please pray this prayer:

Lord Jesus, I need You. I want You. I know I am a sinner. I am sorry for my sins. Thank You for dying on the cross for my sins. I believe You are the Son of God. Wash my sins away by Your blood. I welcome Your Holy Spirit into my heart. As best as I know how, I give You my life. Amen.

Dear reader, the second coming of Jesus Christ is at hand. This means that the Midnight Cry is coming even sooner. It will result in the church all over the globe coming out of their deep slumber. The awakened church will see a restoration of the signs, wonders, and miracles as in the Book of Acts. Millions will be saved, including Muslims and Jews all over the world. The knowledge of the glory of the Lord will indeed cover the earth as the waters cover the sea (Hab. 2:14).

May the grace of our Lord Jesus Christ and the tender mercy of God the Father and the blessing of the Holy Spirit be with you, now and forever. Amen.

NOTES

INTRODUCTION

1. Henry Alford, *The New Testament for English Readers*, vol. 1 (Cambridge: Deighton, Bell, and Co., 1868), 172.

CHAPTER 1
ISHMAEL

1. Vinson Synan, "Pentecostalism: William Seymour," *Christianity Today*, accessed May 9, 2016, http://www.christianitytoday.com/history/issues/issue-65 /pentecostalism-william-seymour.html; Leonard Lovett, "William J. Seymour: Peril and Possibilities for a New Era," *Enrichment Journal*, accessed May 9, 2016, http://enrichmentjournal.ag.org/200602/200602_046_Seymour.cfm.

2. Vinson Synan, *An Eyewitness Remembers the Century of the Holy Spirit* (Grand Rapids, MI: Chosen Books, 2010), 21; "William Seymour and the History of the Azusa Street Outpouring," Revival Library, accessed May 9, 2016, http://www.revival-library.org/pensketches/am_pentecostals/seymourazusa.html.

3. "Bishop William J. Seymour," AzusaStreet.org, accessed May 9, 2016, http://www.azusastreet.org/WilliamJSeymour.htm.

4. "George Jeffreys 1889–1962," SmithWigglesworth.com, accessed May 10, 2016, http://www.smithwigglesworth.com/pensketches/jeffreysg.htm; "Stephen Jeffreys 1876–1943," SmithWigglesworth.com, accessed May 10, 2016, http:// www.smithwigglesworth.com/pensketches/jeffreyss.htm.

5. Bill Sherman, "Religion: Tulsa Called Key City in Religious Movements," *Tulsa World*, October 7, 2013, accessed May 9, 2016, http://www.tulsaworld.com /archives/religion-tulsa-called-key-city-in-religious-movements/article_7ba23e00 -d73a-54dd-b2bb-217d467f5c05.html.

CHAPTER 2
ISAAC

1. Smith Wigglesworth gave this prophecy in 1947.

2. George Stormont, *Smith Wigglesworth: A Man Who Walked With God* (Tulsa, OK: Harrison House, 1989), 123.

CHAPTER 7
THE SLEEPING CHURCH

1. As quoted in Peyton Jones, "In His Absence," *Leadership Journal*, September 2015, accessed June 23, 2016, http://www.christianitytoday.com/le/2015 /september-web-exclusive/in-his-absence.html.

2. As quoted in Larry Crabb, "Lesson Three: A Personal Search: Beginning With an Inside Look," *SoulCare Foundations I: The Basic Model*, course study guide, 31, updated 2015, Our Daily Bread Christian University, accessed June 23, 2016, https://dpz73qkr83w0p.cloudfront.net/en_US/course_study_guide/CC201.pdf.

3. Kevin Turner, "Why Isn't the American Church Experiencing Revival?," CharismaMag.com, January 8, 2013, accessed May 10, 2016, http://www.charismamag.com/spirit/revival/1474-why-isnt-the-american-church-growing.

CHAPTER 8
COMMON GRACE,
ISRAEL, AND A SLEEPING WORLD

1. Michael Youssef, *God, Help Me Overcome My Circumstances* (Eugene, OR: Harvest House Publishers, 2015), 44.

2. Ibid., 44–46.

3. Ibid., 46.

4. Ibid., 46–47.

5. Ibid., 47.

6. Jared Wilson, "They Will Know You Are Conference Christians by Your Porn?," The Gospel Coalition, April 10, 2015, accessed June 24, 2016, https://blogs.thegospelcoalition.org/gospeldrivenchurch/2015/04/10/they-will-know-you-are-conference-christians-by-your-porn/.

CHAPTER 11
THE MESSAGE

1. John Paul Jackson shared the details of his vision with me in 2001.

CHAPTER 12
THE MESSENGERS

1. John Paul Jackson shared the details of his vision with me in 2001.

CHAPTER 13
THE AWAKENED CHURCH

1. Burk Parsons, "Give Me Scotland, or I Die," Ligonier Ministries, March 1, 2014, accessed June 28, 2016, http://www.ligonier.org/learn/articles/give-me-scotland-or-i-die/.

2. Dan Graves, "John Wesley's Heart Strangely Warmed," Church History Timeline: 1701–1800, updated April 2007, accessed June 28, 2016, http://www.christianity.com/church/church-history/timeline/1701-1800/john-wesleys-heart-strangely-warmed-11630227.html.

CHAPTER 16
THIS SAME JESUS

1. John Calvin, *Calvin's Commentaries*, Acts 7, BibleHub.com, accessed June 29, 2016, http://biblehub.com/commentaries/calvin/acts/7.htm.

2. "Polycarp Refuses to Revile Christ," in *The Apostolic Fathers With Justin Martyr and Irenaeus*, Christian Classics Ethereal Library, accessed June 29, 2016, http://www.ccel.org/ccel/schaff/anf01.iv.iv.ix.html.

3. Michelle A. Vu, "Rick Warren Clarifies Doctrine, Purpose Driven Life with John Piper—TRANSCRIPT," *The Christian Post*, May 28, 2011, accessed June 28, 2016, http://www.christianpost.com/news/transcript-john-piper-rick-warren-on-doctrine-purpose-driven-life-50615/.

4. "Since Jesus Came Into My Heart" by R. H. McDaniel. Public domain.

CHAPTER 20
THE PURPOSE OF THE SECOND COMING

1. Augustine, "On Man's Perfection in Righteousness," in Philip Schaff, ed., *Nicene and Post-Nicene Fathers, First Series*, vol. 5, trans. by Peter Holmes and Robert Ernest Wallis (Buffalo, NY: Christian Literature Publishing Co., 1887), revised and edited for New Advent, accessed June 30, 2016, http://www.newadvent.org/fathers/1504.htm.

2. Athanasius, "Statement of Faith," in Philip Schaff, ed., *Nicene and Post-Nicene Fathers, Second Series*, vol. 4, trans. by Archibald Robertson (Buffalo, NY: Christian Literature Publishing Co., 1892), revised and edited for New Advent, accessed June 30, 2016, http://www.newadvent.org/fathers/2821.htm.

3. "XXVIII. Exhortation to Prayer," in William Cowper, *Poems, Vol. 2* (Boston: E. Lincoln, 1802), 31.

CONNECT WITH US!

CHARISMA HOUSE

(Spiritual Growth)

f Facebook.com/CharismaHouse

🐦 @CharismaHouse

📷 Instagram.com/CharismaHouseBooks

SILOAM

(Health)

📌 Pinterest.com/CharismaHouse

REALMS

(Fiction)

f Facebook.com/RealmsFiction